VOGUE

EASY SEWING

VOGUE

EASY SEWING

HARPER & ROW, PUBLISHERS, NEW YORK

Cambridge, Philadelphia, San Francisco, London
Mexico City, São Paulo, Singapore, Sydney

Writer: *Lynn C. Ferrari*
Illustrator: *Phoebe Adams Gaughan*
Editor: *Helen Moore*
Coordinator for Butterick: *Patricia Perry*
Butterick staff: *Jane Glanzer, Carol Sharma, Renee Ullman, Ron Ferguson*
Coordinator for Harper & Row: *Carol Cohen*
Harper & Row production staff: *Mary Chadwick, Lydia Link, Coral Tysliava*

VOGUE EASY SEWING. Copyright © 1985 by Butterick Company, Inc. All rights reserved. Printed in the United States of America. No part of this book may be used or
reproduced in any manner whatsoever without written permission except in the
case of brief quotations embodied in critical articles and reviews. For information
address Harper & Row, Publishers, Inc., 10 East 53rd Street, New York, N.Y. 10022.
Published simultaneously in Canada by Fitzhenry & Whiteside Limited, Toronto.

FIRST EDITION

Designed by Jos. Trautwein/Bentwood Studio

Library of Congress Cataloging in Publication Data

Main entry under title:

Vogue easy sewing.

Includes index.
1. Dressmaking.   2. Sewing.
TT515.V622   1985   646.4'304   84-48531
ISBN 0-06-181128-9 (U.S.A. and Canada)
ISBN 0-06-337041-7 (outside U.S.A. and Canada)

85 86 87 88 89   10 9 8 7 6 5 4 3 2 1

Other books from Vogue:

VOGUE SEWING
VOGUE CHRISTMAS
VOGUE FITTING

CONTENTS

The Art
of
Easy Sewing

Easy sewing is as much a philosophy as it is a series of quick techniques and simplified methods. It's being organized and efficient with your time, space and systems. Easy sewing also is knowing what patterns, fabrics and notions work best for you and save you time as you sew. It's knowing what your sewing machine and other tools can and can't do, and even the right height for your chair! The more you develop and personalize your own easy sewing philosophy, the more easily you'll be able to sew!

Easy Wardrobe Planning

You never should buy or sew anything without a plan. If you impulse buy, you inevitably end up with garments that neither add to nor build on clothes you already have. This is an expensive and limiting way to dress! Therefore, before you sew another thing, take time out to analyze your personal style and the clothes and accessories already in your closet. The results of your study will be the sewing and buying plan for meeting your wardrobe needs.

First, in a leotard or slip, do a self-study. Really look at your neck, shoulders, bust, rib cage, arms, stomach, waist, abdomen, hips, buttocks and legs. Pinpoint your best attributes, your so-so features and your worst figure flaws. Take notes.

Now, go "shopping," *without* cash, a credit card or a checkbook. Try on clothes in all the categories that match the categories of your life . . . office clothes, exercise clothes, evening clothes and so on. If you've always been strictly tailored, try a blouse with a bow at the neck. If you've worn nothing but ruffles for years, try strictly tailored. Compare your opinion of the style, on you, with your self-study notes. If your shoulders are not at the top of your "best" list, select things that either conceal or flatter the flaw. Learn to spot the styles that make them look their very worst, too. If, on the other hand, your shoulders rate high on the list, try on more clothes that show them to their best advantage. Check the best hem length for your proportions and legs, the best waistline placement, bodice fit and sleeve length, too. Also observe new colors and textures and what they do or don't do for you. Again, take notes and make a list.

What you have, when you're finished, is a comprehensive understanding of the clothes that help you look your very best and those that do absolutely nothing for you, even though you love them. On your next shopping trip—through a pattern catalog—you'll not be tempted to buy a single pattern that will become a garment hanging in the back of your closet because it's unflattering!

The final stop in your wardrobe planning tour is *your* closet. Take everything out of it and arrange piles of like items . . . skirts, blouses, pants, jackets, and so on.

- *Pull out a favorite staple, such as a jacket or blazer.*
- *With an eye to color, fabric weight and texture, pull out all the bottoms that look like they may combine well with it.*
- *Add the shirts, blouses and sweaters that might coordinate, too.*
- *Try on all the combinations and make note of the ones that work.*
- *Begin again with another staple, such as a skirt, finding all the tops that combine to make multiple outfits.*
- *Add accessories . . . sometimes the only thing a new combination needs is a belt to make it work!*

It's a good idea to have a friend help you do this. She can spot combinations you wouldn't think of trying because her viewpoint is fresher. She's not limited by thinking in terms of what items you've always worn together, the way you may be.

What you'll have is threefold: First, ensembles that work in multiple ways; second, pieces that would work but have a missing element; and third, rejects—things that look awful or work with nothing else.

What you have, too, is your immediate wardrobe plan for future sewing projects! You know, now, if you need a navy skirt that would work with two different jackets and three different blouses to give you six new coordinated looks, and you know if you need a neutral jacket that would give a new look to a dress plus work wonderfully with two skirts and a pair of pants you already own. Developing a color theme in your wardrobing is an excellent way to plan to sew garments that multiply and combine with more and more pieces.

This is your wardrobe plan *and* your sewing plan. To facilitate future fabric shopping and matching, develop a system of keeping a record of fabrics you have already used. If you made many of the clothes in your closet, locate scraps and cut swatches. If no swatches are available, take the garment to be coordinated with you, instead.

Easy Pattern Selection

Wardrobe building is a lot easier if you know not only what style but also what type of pattern to buy. Easy-to-sew patterns that combine up-to-the-minute fashion with easy construction techniques are the perfect solution as your sewing time becomes more and more limited.

Look for patterns that have a minimum of seams, designer details and pattern pieces. Study the fashion illustrations and backviews, and read the back of the envelope to check for these elements. Avoid multiple pleats, bias skirts and welt pockets, for example. They may require more time than you have to spare. Go ahead when you spot dolman or raglan sleeves, mock bands, narrow hems, elasticized waists, unlined styles and few or no buttonholes.

Although not stated, most easy patterns limit garment construction to flat construction methods whenever possible. Not only are they easier, but they are faster, too. Each section of a garment is completed before the major seams are stitched together, since sleeves, zippers, pockets, facings, bands, and topstitching all can be executed more easily when the garment is still flat.

Also look for patterns with minimal or loose fit, although *good* fit is integral to good fashion. To facilitate correcting any fit problems you may have, multi-size patterns are an excellent choice. A combination of sizes is included on one pattern tissue, so if you are one size on top and another on the bottom, you can make adjustments simply by drawing new connecting lines along the cutting lines, right on the pattern! If you've never used a multi-size pattern, it may look different than the patterns you've used in the past. Once you begin to work with it, however, you'll see how easy it is to follow the cutting lines for your size or sizes. To make the pattern easier to use, there are no stitching lines printed on the pattern tissue. Since seams are usually 5/8" (15mm) (if not, it's noted on the pattern tissue), it's easy to mark them before cutting if you prefer, or to simply follow the stitching guide on your sewing machine.

Once you've used a pattern, think about how you can use it again. If you make a black wool skirt, and love it, make it in black linen for spring. Familiarity with that pattern makes sewing even faster the second time around! In fact, if you've used a pattern once, make it twice the second time. If you make it in two comparable fabric weights, in the same predominant color, you can cut out and stitch two as you go without even having to change the thread.

Fabric Dos and Don'ts

Always look for quality and easy handling when selecting fabrics that will be easy to sew. Even the bargain prices of sleazy, flawed or off-grain fabrics are not enough to offset the serious sewing problems you'll encounter.

To be able to utilize easy construction methods, choose fabrics that are firmly woven or knitted, with body and resiliency, and that don't require a lining or an underlining. Fabrics without nap, a one-way design or a matching pattern are easier to lay out, and fabrics that do not ravel will not need seam finishes . . . all definite timesavers! Some examples of easy-sew fabrics are double knits, broadcloth, gabardine, flannel, seersucker, poplin and corduroy.

In addition to avoiding poor quality, at any cost, it is best to avoid fabrics that require special handling, techniques and methods, only because they take extra time. Such fabrics as satin, matte jersey, chiffon and charmeuse are delicate and slippery—factors that call for special attention. Real leather and suede, deep-pile fabrics and fake fur require special techniques and tools, and lace and very stretchy knits are also handled differently than most other fabrics.

It's much easier to take creative sewing shortcuts when you follow the basic, easy wardrobe, pattern and fabric guidelines. It's also easier when you organize as many sewing elements as you can, from the space you use to the tools you select.

Sewing Time

Organize your sewing time so it works for you. Determine the steps that take *you* the longest to complete and plan them around your largest blocks of available uninterrupted time. If you have to clear the decks and the dining room or kitchen table to lay out and cut out patterns, try to cut out more than one at a time—the pattern you're working on first, and the one you have for later, too. This way you don't have to take time to clear everything away again when you're ready for your second project.

Once you have your work space prepared, try to complete the layout/cutout work at one sitting. If you segment this portion of sewing, you usually have to rethink, re-measure and reconsider such things as grain, basic fit adjustments and cutting lines. This not only takes extra time, it makes the task less than easy.

Use non-sewing time to complete handwork. Portable projects, such as hems, finishing work and buttons, are done easily when you are commuting and waiting for appointments and are a great way to make telephone talking and television watching productive. Nowhere is it mandated that this part of sewing must be done in your sewing area. Try to utilize otherwise "spare" time for these steps. To accomplish this easily, create a portable sewing kit. The only elements that change are the thread and notions you need for your current project. The rest of the kit, which can be a basket, plastic bag or tote bag, should include:

- *scissors*
- *thread clipper*
- *wrist pincushion*
- *pins*
- *needles*
- *thimble*
- *ruler*
- *tape measure*
- *"garbage" bag*

Consider the kit as essential as your handbag and take it everywhere you go, with the portion of the garment on which you're working. It's amazing how much hand sewing you can accomplish in small amounts of non-sewing time, giving yourself more concentrated sewing time at your machine.

Use your sewing time to your best advantage and develop a comfortable system. One suggestion is to sew all darts, for example, before pressing. Then sew all the seams you can, on all pieces. This saves the need to go back and forth constantly from sewing machine to iron every time you complete one step. Combine steps to save time!

Make your shopping time more fun by keeping your "inventory" of finished garments, fabric yardage, notions and patterns in an easy-to-find format:

- *Keep swatches on a giant safety pin or in a purse-size photo album. Mark each one with the yardage you have on hand to facilitate pattern selection.*

- *Make your own pattern catalog. Make photocopies of your pattern envelopes, front and back, and file them by category (blouses, skirts, etc.) behind tabs in a looseleaf notebook. Pin on swatches of the fabric you used or plan to use. You now have a complete record of yardage and notion information and fabrics with which you can coordinate new purchases.*

- *Keep a list of notions you need and take it with you when you shop to avoid returning for the one thing you always forget when you don't use a list!*

Sewing Space

With the exception of layout/cutout space, which often indeed is your kitchen or dining table or a board on the bed or the floor, your sewing space should be organized, accessible and as set up as you possibly can make it. The greatest obstacle to easy sewing is having to drag out all your gear and set it up just to begin!

It would be wonderful, of course, to have an entire room to use for sewing and be able to close the door at the end of a session without picking up or putting away a thing. This is a luxury few sewers have, however, so a sewing space or sewing area is the alternative. Your sewing space does not have to be any less wonderful than a whole room would be, and often can be more efficient.

SEWING ERGONOMICS

Making your sewing area conform to *your* form, rather than the other way around, is a primary consideration. This principle is called ergonomics and is used by furniture and equipment designers who want business furniture that creates comfort and efficiency and eliminates fatigue, stress and discomfort. They know more is accomplished if the workers aren't distracted by aching backs and necks! Sewing is easier and more fun, too, if you don't end a session suffering a stiff neck, a sore back, tired arms or strained eyes. A sewer's lament, all too often, is a listing of these ailments after a concentrated period of sewing.

Your Chair

The chair you use should be the right height for you. The distance from the seat to the floor should be about two inches less than the distance from the back of your knee to the floor. This height keeps your thighs from resting heavily against the chair, a position that compresses blood vessels and nerves in your legs and causes them to go to sleep. If you're not in the market for a new chair right now, you can adjust your leg position by placing a platform or block of wood on the floor. The platform needs to be big enough to accommodate both your feet and your sewing machine foot control. If the foot control slips, glue a carpet remnant to the platform.

The chair seat should tilt slightly to the back so you aren't shifting and sliding as you sew. The seat also should be proportional to you from front to back, so your back can lean against the chair back without the front edge cutting into the backs of your knees.

Ideally, the chair also should be a swivel chair that rolls so

you can wheel yourself from machine to ironing board without constantly popping up and down.

Lighting

Good sewing lighting should be glare-free and bright. Indirect lighting or direct lighting slightly in front of your work minimizes reflection, shadows and glare, all of which cause your eyes to get tired faster and cause strain. For the few times you need reflection, such as when you're sewing with shiny, dark thread on a dark, matte fabric, reposition the light until it gives you the contrast you need. A clamp-on desk lamp or goose-neck lamp is particularly good, since you can move it to direct light where you need it. Of course, take advantage of natural light whenever you can.

Work Surfaces

Work at counters or tabletops that allow you to keep your elbows down. The higher you have to lift your arms to cut, sew or iron, the more rapidly you will get tired. If you stand to cut or iron, waist-high usually is the correct level for your work surface.

The way you place your sewing tools in your sewing area helps eliminate strain and fatigue, too. Again, a swivel chair is a plus, since you're twisting it instead of your back!

Making your sewing space as body-efficient as possible is a key factor in planning a totally efficient sewing space. Other considerations, such as the way

you refer to the pattern instruction sheet and what you do about snipped threads and fabric scraps, all contribute to the way you can make sewing easy.

SEWING AREAS

Because of your busy schedule, your sewing time may be fragmented. Your goal should be to be able to sit right down, turn on the light, plug in the machine and sew. Even if you have only a few minutes, you can accomplish a tremendous amount if everything is at the ready. Whether your sewing space is an entire room or a small sewing area, it should be set up so that everything is where you expect it to be and easy to reach.

Think about it as you would your kitchen. You don't keep the cooking tools you use most frequently, like spatulas, wooden spoons and pot holders, on a shelf you need to stand on a stool to get to! Neither should your most frequently used sewing equipment be stored in hard-to-reach places.

There are several alternatives for creating your sewing area. There are specially designed units and cabinets that are manufactured to be sewing centers. They have spaces and places for storing your notions and tools. When the unit is closed, everything is hidden away and your dining room or bedroom reverts to its primary function.

Another option is to take over two feet of space along an entire wall and enclose it with cabinet or louver doors. When the doors are open, the counter, sewing and storage spaces are work-ready. When they're

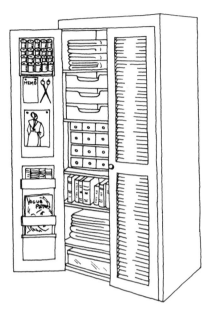

zipper color or machine accessory you need.

- Use a baby food lazy susan (available at most children's toy and furniture stores) for notions storage. If you aren't using baby food in your household, ask a friend who is to save jars for you. Washed and de-labeled, they are see-through containers that give you what you need at a spin!

- Multi-drawer plastic cases that hardware stores carry for screws, nuts, washers and bolts also are excellent for button storage. Color-code each drawer with a self-stick label and colored pencil for easy reference.

- If you cut out or work on more than one project at a time, giant self-locking plastic bags keep fabric, pattern and notions clean

and together, as a unit, ready to pull out when you're ready for them, and easy to see.

- Pegboards become invaluable when outfitted with hardware store accessories—long pegs for thread spools; clear plastic jars that screw into hook-on lids for buttons, snaps, safety pins and hooks and eyes; curved hooks for hanging scissors and shears—all keep like things neat, together and handy.

- A bulletin board hung slightly above and in front of your machine gives you easy eye contact with the pattern instruction sheet and with your sewing machine instruction manual when you're trying a new technique.

- A full-length mirror in your sewing area needn't be expensive but saves you expensive mis-

closed, they form an attractive wall.

Modular units can be assembled to handle your sewing equipment. Most have slide-out or pull-down desk or table surfaces for your machine. The machine slides back in for storage, and the table folds back up to conceal it.

If you simply do not have an inch of wall space or a corner to give up to a sewing area, then convert an existing shelf unit or bureau for organized storage and keep your most-used accessories in a portable basket to carry to your machine.

Organizing Tips

- Visibility is especially important. Clear plastic boxes and bags save minutes of precious time wasted if you have to root through shoe boxes to find the

takes. You can try on as you sew and easily check fit, length and appearance without guessing how you look from the back or side. It also saves you time, since you won't have to dash to another room to see yourself every time you need to check, and it's efficient—no more standing on a chair in front of the medicine cabinet mirror to look at a hem length!

- Set up your ironing board at sitting height right in your sewing area, so you can press as you sew without taking extra steps. A small travel board or sleeve board is a good accessory.

- A waste receptacle is a must so your sewing surface isn't cluttered with litter. If you haven't room for a wastebasket, tape a small paper bag to the base of your machine or the edge of the table and sweep trimmings into it as you sew.

- Wear a wrist pincushion or strap a pincushion stitched to elastic around the head of your sewing machine to keep pins from scattering over your work surface as you sew. Or use a flat magnet with an adhesive backing to stick onto your sewing machine bed.

- When pins spill, use a large magnet for a quick pickup.

- Glue a small magnet to one end of a yardstick for easy, right-from-your-chair gathering of pins that have fallen on the floor.

- Keep your patterns filed on end, with the pattern numbers on top. If you just can't get them back into the envelopes after you've used them, keep them self-contained in small self-locking bags. For fast reference, keep like patterns together, by category—dresses, crafts, jackets, skirts, etc.

- Pocket file folders also become good pattern storage. Write the pattern number on the file tab, cut and paste the envelope front and back to the file folder and keep the patterns, by category, in a file box or cabinet.

- Fabric should be organized, too. Take a little time and measure and mark your yardage so you don't have to re-measure it every time you're thinking of using it for a project. Keep it rolled on bolts to prevent wrinkles and save extra ironing time. Ask the manager of your favorite fabric store to save empty bolts for you.

- Even your remnants can be put in good order! Eliminate the chaos of a scrap basket and measure and file like remnants together in self-locking plastic bags. Include notes and ideas for future use so doll clothes, patchwork squares or contrast pockets or trim are easy to find, at a glance.

- Buy fusible interfacing on sale, and keep it rolled on wrapping paper tubes to prevent wrinkling and for easy roll-out when you need it.

The easier it is to work in your sewing area, the easier sewing is. Comfort, organized space, organized equipment and materials and time- and energy-saving methods all help you to sew more than you ever have before, even if you have less time than you would like.

Easy Sewing Essentials

Another aid to easy sewing is having the right equipment for the task at hand. Just as it's much easier to cut up a chicken with poultry shears than with a paring knife, it's also easier to cut out a skirt pattern with sharp, bent-handled dressmaker's shears than with small, dull scissors. There's an ever-growing range of tools, notions, aids and equipment available, and it's a sewer's dream come true to own them all. But even owning a few tools that meet your immediate sewing needs, to begin, can make your sewing time efficient and much, much easier.

To save time, store your equipment by category. Keep all your marking tools together, for example. Measuring tools, cutting tools and pressing aids, when kept together, by category, are easy to find and help you establish good work habits—you'll always use the right tool at the proper time instead of grabbing the first thing you find, which may not be suited for the job, because you can't find the correct tool.

Keep your equipment in good condition. Throw out pins and needles that are dull or have nicks or burrs so they can't cause snags or skipped stitches. Mark scissors and shears—shears that cut paper get dulled and should not be used to cut fabric. Keep them sharp. Sewing isn't easy if your equipment can't do the job it's supposed to do.

MEASURING TOOLS

The best result of easy sewing is having something you love to wear when you're finished. You won't love a garment in beautiful fabric, perfectly made, if it doesn't fit. Good-quality measuring tools, used often and accurately, help you obtain the fit you need. Fast sewing does *not* mean guessing how much three inches is!

Tape measures should be 60" (152cm) long, with metal tips. They should be made of a non-stretch material for complete accuracy and have the numbers, in inches or centimeters, printed on both sides.

Rulers should have metal edges or be made of see-through plastic. You should have one that is 12" to 18" (30.5cm to 46cm) long and one that is 5" to 6" (12.5cm to 15cm) long.

Yardsticks, which measure 36" (91.5cm), are excellent for checking fabric grainline, measuring the length of altered pattern pieces, marking hem lengths and other general marking. They should be made of metal or shellacked hardwood. New yardsticks have inches and centimeters on opposite edges of both sides.

Sewing gauges are 6" (15cm) plastic or metal rulers that have a sliding indicator. They provide fast and accurate measurements of hems, buttonholes, seam allowances and pleats.

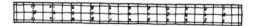

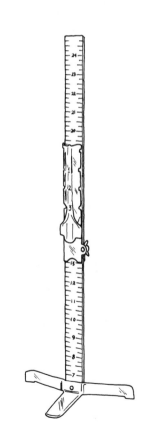

A **T-square,** an essential tool for drafters and engineers, is a good friend to sewers, too. Use it to straighten grain, locate opposite grains, alter pattern tissue and for other marking processes.

A **French curve** becomes an easy-sewing tool when you use it as a guide for re-drawing curved areas such as necklines and armholes when altering patterns, and when connecting cutting lines for different sizes on multi-size patterns. It may be made of metal or plastic and is sharply curved on one side with a straight measure on the other side.

A **skirt marker** gives you an easy way to measure hems. Pin markers are the most accurate, but they require two people. You can use a chalk marker by yourself, but test your fabric first—chalk does not come out of all fabrics. Combination markers are available. Be sure the marker you buy is adjustable to all hem lengths.

23

MARKING TOOLS

Most sewers list marking as their greatest complaint. They hate to take the time to mark when what they really want to do is start sewing! Breakthroughs in this category, however, have made it much easier, and having the right tools speeds the process. One type of marking tool may not work on all fabrics, so it's best to make a small investment in different kinds.

Tracing paper is one easy way to transfer pattern construction marks to fabric. It can be carbon-coated on one side, for marking one layer of fabric, or on both sides, for marking two layers at once. Tracing paper now comes in packages of three to five colors. One caveat—pretest it for permanency on your fabric. Even though most tracing paper marks are removable by washing or dry cleaning, they can become permanent, on some fabrics, if they are pressed *before* cleaning.

Tracing wheels, the natural partners of tracing paper, have either serrated or smooth edges. The serrated wheel leaves a dotted line and is suitable for most fabrics. The smooth wheel makes a firm, solid line and is good for heavily textured and delicate fabrics.

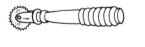

Tailor's chalk has undergone modernization and comes with several different kinds of handles and holders that keep your hands and the chalk clean. Many have built-in sharpeners and erasers. They mark only one layer of fabric at a time. Most chalk refills are available in packages of three colors. Avoid marking chalk or pencils made of wax—they leave greasy stains when the marks are pressed.

Marking pencils, usually available in yellow, pink, blue or white, are made like wooden pencils and are designed to fit any pencil sharpener, so you can hone as sharp a point as you need. Most have brush erasers for removing marks.

Marking pens are the newest invention to be perfected to make sewing preparation easier. The marks either fade away within twenty-four to forty-eight hours, disappear when gently touched by a damp cloth or wash out, depending on the brand. With these pens you now can mark on the right side of the fabric without trepidation . . . by all means, pre-test on your fabric if the very thought makes you nervous!

CUTTING TOOLS

When you stitch along the stitching line, the finished seam will only be as accurate as you cut the original cutting line. There's nothing easy about sewing with precision if the fabric you cut out lacks even edges and true curves. For this reason, shop carefully for shears and scissors.

- *Look for steel or molybdenum coated with nickel, for protection, and chrome-plated, to prevent rusting.*

- *Scissors and shears should cut sharply, not just at the point but all the way to the back of the blades, too. Test them before you buy them. If they catch a thread of the fabric, the cutting blades are imperfect.*

- *An adjustable screw feature in shears allows you to adjust them to your particular feel. Cutting tools with rivets may loosen and cannot be tightened.*

- *If you're left-handed, buy left-handed shears.*

Take good care of your scissors and shears and they'll last a lifetime. Periodically oil the screw section with sewing machine oil, then wipe off excess oil with a soft cloth. The first time you use your shears after oiling, cut on scraps of fabric before cutting your fashion fabric. Keep them sharp, and never dull them by cutting paper heavier than tissue; have a separate pair of paper scissors on hand instead.

Equally as important as good quality is having the right tool for the job. Those listed here are the essentials . . . there are several others for special cutting jobs that are nice to have but not mandatory for your easy-sewing projects.

Bent-handled dressmaker's shears are designed for cutting fabric so the fabric rests flat while being cut. They are most widely available in four lengths from 7" to 10" (18cm to 25.5cm) and also in various weights. Choose the length and weight that's comfortable for you to use with accuracy. The two handles are shaped differently—hold them with the oval-shaped handle on the bottom. Some have a serrated edge that adds control for cutting lightweight and slippery fabrics.

Pinking or scalloping shears are used to finish raw edges of fabrics that do not ravel easily. Pinking shears give a zigzag cut; scalloping shears, a rounded cut. Each is available in several lengths and weights. They feel stiffer to use than regular shears; some will be more comfortable than others. Test for comfort and smooth cutting on various scraps of the fabric type you use most often.

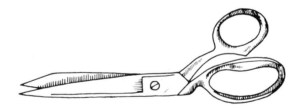

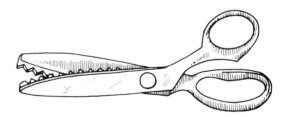

Sewing scissors are used for trimming, clipping and delicate cutting. In contrast to shears, scissors are straight and have identical round handles. Found most readily in 5″ and 6″ lengths (12.5cm and 15cm) with pointed ends, some may have one blunt point to prevent snagging fabric.

Seam rippers are simple, small, penlike and very, very sharp. Use them, carefully, for fast ripping of mistakes. The one protected point slides into the seam and lifts the threads to be cut by the curved blade.

Electric scissors are essential for sewers who have difficulty manipulating shears or who have arthritis. They are available in one or two speeds. Some have cords; others are battery operated.

Rotary cutters also are especially good for sewers with hand ailments. They are operated by the same principle as a tracing wheel, rolling forward and backward along straight lines and curves with quick, smooth cutting accuracy. Since rotary cutters are very sharp, they should be used with a specially-designed cutting board. The board protects your table or other surface you may be using for cutting.

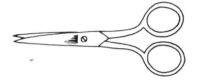

Buttonhole scissors are designed to cut open buttonholes accurately and can be adjusted by a screw and nut for different buttonhole lengths.

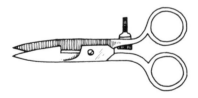

Thread clips fit neatly into your hand, with a ring for your little finger. They have an inner spring mechanism to keep them apart until you squeeze with the palm of your hand. They snip stray threads neatly and easily and, if they are very sharp, can make the small clips needed for marking or for curved seams, too.

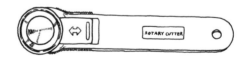

STITCHING TOOLS

Many a beautiful fabric has been ruined by the hurried use of the wrong pin or needle. Knowing what to use need not be complicated, and the needle and thread chart on page 31 should serve as your ready reference. Reaching for the right pin for the fabric you're using is easy if you keep separate pincushions or boxes for each type. Many pincushions have an attached emery bag (often a little strawberry) for sharpening and removing rust from pins and needles.

Pins are classified according to metal type, diameter and length. They should be rustproof, and preferably made of brass or stainless steel. Uncoated steel pins can rust, and nickel-plated steel pins sometimes leave a black mark on some fabrics. Do not stitch over pins because they can break sewing machine needles.

Pins with glass or plastic ball heads are good for pinning patterns to fabric because they're easy to see and pick up.

Standard pins have flat heads, and T-pins, which are shaped like their name, are good with deep-pile, loosely woven and bulky knitted fabrics, as their shape keeps them from slipping through the fabric.

The diameter of a pin corresponds to its length. Generally, the longer the pin, the thicker it is. The shortest, smallest-diameter or finest pin is a silk pin. The next smallest diameter pin is a dressmaker pin, which is the one most commonly used for home sewing. Pin size is stated in sixteenths of an inch, according to length. For example, a No. 16 pin is 16/16" or 1" (25mm) long. The dressmaker pin, No. 17, is 17/16" or 1-1/16" (26mm) long. Match your pin choice to the fabric you're using, following your common sense . . . long pins with large diameters obviously would not be suitable for delicate fabrics but are perfect for heavy or loosely woven fabrics, which they can hold and in which they wouldn't leave any marks. Ballpoint pins (without a sharp point) don't work on finely woven fabrics but are ideal for knits because they slip between yarns without poking or snagging.

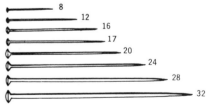

Hand needles also are classified according to type and size, but, unlike pins, the largest needles have the smallest numbers. For general hand sewing they range from 1, the largest, to 12, the smallest. Sizes 5 to 10 take care of most of your dressmaking needs.

Needles also have names:

When you're matching the needle to your need, consider fabric structure, weight and thread thickness. A needle should be fine enough to slip easily through fabric yet strong enough that it doesn't break or bend. Generally, the finer or more sheer the fabric, the sharper and more slender the

- **Sharps** *are medium length, have a round eye and are suitable for almost all fabric weights.*

- **Calyx-eye** *(self-threading) needles have a slot rather than a round eye, but otherwise are just like sharps.*

- **Betweens** *are shorter than sharps, have round eyes and are good for taking fine stitches in fabrics.*

- **Milliners** *are longer than sharps and betweens and can take long, quick basting stitches with ease.*

- **Ball-point** *needles resemble sharps but have a rounded point to penetrate between knit yarns.*

needle should be. Needles are sold in packets; assorted or the same type and size together. It's best to store them in their marked packets for easy reference.

There is a range of other needles designed for other kinds of sewing, too, from darning to sail making, but none of them is a sewing essential as you get your sewing area organized.

Sewing machine needles should be chosen with both thread size and fabric type in mind. They should be fine enough to penetrate fabric without snagging or marring it, with a large enough eye that the thread doesn't fray when it's pulled through it. They must also be strong enough not to bend or break. Needles have different points.

- *Regular, sharp needles are suitable for all woven fabrics.*

- *Ball-point needles, like ball-point pins and hand-sewing needles, have a rounded point that pushes between fabric yarns instead of through them. Use them for knits and elastic fabrics.*

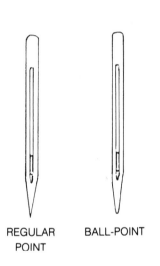

REGULAR POINT   BALL-POINT

Needle sizes are standard but can have either American or metric numbers. Refer to the following chart for equivalents. Sewing machine needles are numbered in the opposite direction from hand-sewing needles; here the finest size, 9, has the lowest number and the largest size, 18, has the highest number. Sizes 11 and 14 are used the most often for general sewing.

EQUIVALENT SEWING MACHINE NEEDLE SIZES

American	9	11	14	16	18
Metric	70	80	90	100	110

29

Understanding how a sewing machine needle is designed saves time when you're changing and inserting needles. Usually, the top portion is rounded on one side and flat on the other. The lower portion has a groove which extends from the top to the eye. This groove guides the thread as it feeds through the needle. When inserting a needle, the groove should face the same direction as the last thread guide above the needle.

Needle threaders are invaluable devices for speeding the process of threading any kind of needle. Simply pull one end of the thread through the very large eye of the threader, insert the threader point through the eye of the needle, pull the thread end out of the threader and remove the threader.

Thread, like fabric, is made of various fibers in various weights. As a general rule, stitch natural fibers with natural threads and synthetic fibers with synthetic fiber thread. Cotton-wrapped polyester thread is the exception and is an all-purpose thread that can be used safely on most fabrics. Also, synthetic threads are best for knits of any fiber content, because of their stretchability.

Some thread is numbered, with the higher numbers denoting finer thread. The midpoint is #50. Sometimes thread size is marked by letters. If this is the case for the thread you buy, remember that A is fine and D is heavy. Special threads are available, too, for quilting, carpets and a range of other projects. Select thread in a shade that matches or is one shade darker than your fabric.

The number of machine stitches you use per inch is the final factor in matching the right stitching tools with your fabric. The following chart gives the general guidelines for combining fabric, thread, needles and stitches for garment construction.

NEEDLE AND THREAD CHART

Uses	Threads		Needles	
Fabric Weight and Type	For All Fabrics	For Natural Fiber Fabrics	Hand	Machine
Very Light* georgette, marquisette, ninon, organdy, organza, net, tulle, lingerie fabrics	Cotton-covered polyester—extra fine Cotton-covered polyester 100% long staple polyester 100% polyester	Mercerized cotton—size 50, 60 Silk—size A	9, 10, 11, 12 Sharps Betweens Milliner's	Finest: 9(70) Stitches per inch: 16–20 per cm: 7–8
Light batiste, voile, lawn, dimity, dotted Swiss, pure silk, crepe de chine*, sheer crepe*, silk jersey*, paper taffeta*, chambray, handkerchief linen, synthetic sheers, cire*, single knits	Cotton-covered polyester—extra fine Cotton-covered polyester 100% long staple polyester 100% polyester	Mercerized cotton—size 50, 60 Silk—size A	9, 10 Sharps Betweens Milliner's	Fine: 9, 11 (70, 80) Stitches per inch: 12–16 per cm: 5–7
Medium Light gingham, challis, percale, sheer wool crepe, peau de soie*, taffeta, pongee, silk surah, wool jersey, cotton knits	Cotton-covered polyester 100% long staple polyester 100% polyester	Mercerized cotton—size 50, 60 Silk—size A	8, 9 Sharps Betweens Milliner's	Fine: 11 (80) Stitches per inch: 12–14 per cm: 5–6
Medium flannel, corduroy, broadcloth, poplin, linen, chintz, muslin, pique, shantung, faille, ottoman, moiré, sharkskin, serge, bouclé, lamé*, velvet*, velveteen, double knits, jacquard knits, velour	Cotton-covered polyester 100% long staple polyester 100% polyester	Mercerized cotton—size 50 Silk—size A	6, 7, 8 Sharps Betweens Milliner's	Medium: 11, 14 (80, 90) Stitches per inch: 12 per cm: 5
Medium Heavy denim, tweed, gabardine, twill, brocade, bengaline, felt, terry, burlap, textured linen, fleece, sweater knits, quilted fabrics	Cotton-covered polyester 100% long staple polyester 100% polyester	Mercerized cotton—size 40, 50 Silk—size A	5, 6 Sharps Betweens Milliner's	Medium Coarse: 14, 16 (90, 100) Stitches per inch: 10–12 per cm: 4–5
Heavy sailcloth, ticking, double-faced wool, heavy coating	Cotton-covered polyester Cotton-covered polyester—extra strong 100% long staple polyester 100% polyester—heavy duty	Mercerized cotton—heavy duty size 40 Silk—size A	4, 5 Sharps Betweens Milliner's	Coarse: 16, 18 (100, 110) Stitches per inch: 8–10 per cm: 3–4

*Fabrics may be more difficult to handle.

Sewing machine attachments are stitching tools that can simplify many time consuming jobs and help make sewing a plea- sure. A seam guide, but- tonholer and zipper foot are attachments to include in the "must have" category.

- *A seam guide attaches to the machine bed and can then be adjusted to a specific distance from the needle. Some machines have markings on the throat plate for the same purpose.*

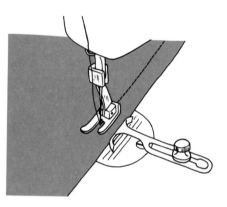

- *A buttonholer quickly and easily stitches buttonholes of the right size for the template or button placed in the attachment. Many machines have a built-in buttonholer which is used with a special foot to make the required size buttonhole.*

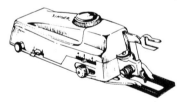

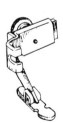

- *A zipper foot is used to stitch close to a raised edge or a seam with more bulk on one side than the other. It is used most often for inserting zippers or for covering and applying piping or cording. To make the stitching of these items easier, the zipper foot is adjustable to the left or right of the needle.*

There are many other attachments that do special sewing jobs fast and professionally, many of which work on all types of machines.

- *An even feed foot feeds both layers of fabric evenly under the needle. It's used for sewing hard-to-feed fabrics, and is also good for stitching plaids, stripes and topstitching.*

- *A roller foot feeds and rolls along with the top layer of fabric so it feeds at the same rate as the bottom layer. The grid on the foot's round, rolling-pin-type rollers prevents the fabric from slipping.*

- *A hemming foot or narrow hemmer evenly turns and stitches a raw edge of fabric in one operation. It works best on lightweight fabrics.*

- *An overedge foot has a metal bar that is placed along the fabric edge so that the machine stitches over the edge. A metal bar holds the fabric in place. It is a good tool for finishing seams and for sewing seams in stretch fabrics.*

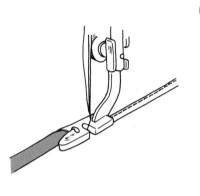

From time to time you may need special attachments for special jobs. Among these are a quilting foot, a button foot, a ruffler, a binder and a special purpose or embroidery foot, each designed to make a particular technique easy.

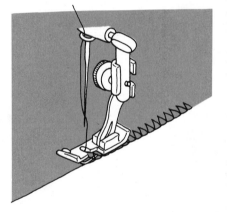

CONSTRUCTION TOOLS

There's the difficult way to do a job, and there's the easy way. Attaching a safety pin to an elastic end and pulling and pushing it through a casing, only to have the pin pop open and get stuck in the middle, is the difficult way. Sticking a pencil into a collar point to turn it out to a sharp corner usually results in a collar with pencil marks showing through from the inside. The easy way is to find the tools that have been designed to do the job fast, neatly and quickly.

Bodkins are easy to use, timesaving devices for drawing elastic, belting and cording through casings. Some work on a pincer principle with small saw teeth, which grip, and a sliding ring, which moves up and tightens the pincers (A). Others have a safety pin closing (B), and a third kind has an eye to thread through (C). Insert the end opposite the holding end into the casing and slide the tool through.

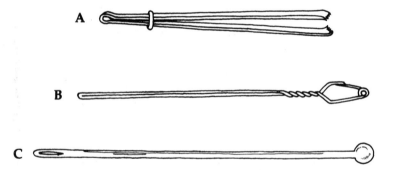

A

B

C

A **pointer and creaser** is a flat wooden tool with one pointed end for pushing out small corners and one rounded end to hold a seam open for pressing.

PRESSING TOOLS

Pressing tools are one of the keys to professionally finished garments. If you press as you sew, you cleanly set and shape stitched lines. A good, adjustable-heat steam iron and an adjustable-height ironing board are the essentials, and there are myriad other accessories that help you press hard-to-reach areas without creasing, flattening or marring the surrounding fabric. A few of them are listed here, with some tips for a homemade variation included! See pages 61–69 for the best pressing techniques.

A **tailor's ham** is a firmly stuffed cushion with rounded surfaces for pressing the shaped and curved areas of your garment, such as darts and sleeve caps. The covering is wool on one side, to quickly absorb and hold steam, and cotton on the other for pressing all fabrics.

A **press mitt** is similar to a tailor's ham but is smaller and has pockets to slip your hand into or to slip over the end of a sleeve board.

A **sleeve board** is a great asset to any sewing area, especially a small one where space is at a premium and you don't have room for a full-size ironing board. It actually is two small ironing boards, attached, on which small seams and details of narrow garment sections can be pressed easily. It folds to store. It should have padding and a silicone cover.

A **seam roll** is a cylindrical cushion, firmly packed, also used for pressing hard-to-reach curved areas and long seams. Because of its rounded shape, you press only the seam and not the surrounding fabric, which prevents ridges or creases from being pressed into the right side. Like the ham, one side is covered with wool, the other with cotton. You can make your own by either covering a tightly rolled magazine with fabric or wrapping a rolling pin with a towel.

Press cloths can be transparent so you can see details and avoid pressing in unwanted creases, or a two-part wool/cotton combination for general pressing. The type you use should be selected in a similiar weight to the weight of your fabric. If you're pressing on the right side, always use a press cloth or use scraps of the garment fabric as a press cloth. Have at least two with your supplies—a transparent or disposable one (available as disposable cloths, sold in packages of three or more) and a two-part wool-and-cotton one, supplementing with scraps of your garment fabric as you need them.

A **point presser** is made of wood and provides many differently shaped surfaces for pressing points, curves and straight edges. The different sizes of curves and narrow straight edges allow you to press seams flat and open without wrinkling the surrounding area. You can use the board as it is for firm fabrics and sharp edges or cover it with a contoured pad for softer edges.

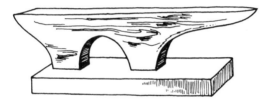

The Practice of Easy Sewing

Mastering the practice of easy sewing really means understanding the best and fastest ways to use your patterns, tools and equipment. It also means understanding the vocabulary and being able to match a method with a name—if your pattern tells you to easestitch and you don't know what that means, you'll be slowed down. The practice of easy sewing can mean Practice Makes Perfect, too. If you've never used fusible interfacing, practice with it **before** you apply it to a garment. Learn how it feels, what it does and how it looks. Then, when you're ready to interface a collar or waistband, you—and it—won't get stuck in the middle! The practice of easy sewing is one case in which familiarity breeds content—the more professional you are at using the wealth of materials designed to make sewing a pleasure, the easier sewing will be.

How to Read
a Pattern Envelope

Since most stores will not let you open a pattern before you buy it, knowing how to read a pattern envelope is an excellent skill to master. Knowing what every word and number means and knowing how to locate the information you need, in a hurry, saves you time and helps avoid purchasing mistakes. As mentioned on page 13, keep construction details in mind when pattern shopping. As a general rule, the less complicated the style, the less complicated the sewing.

PATTERN ENVELOPE FRONT

The envelope front is more than just a pretty picture . . . it's a wealth of information. Whether art illustration or photography is shown, the fashion and technical experts at the pattern companies join forces to make sure that every seam, dart, button, gather and tuck is in precisely the right place, that every sleeve and hem length is exactly where the tissue is marked for it to be, and that every fabric shown is suitable for the construction and style of the garment. As a bonus, the colors and fabrics shown are those most in fashion at the time the pattern is issued. They are available to the sewer "over-the-counter" (not exclusively reserved for ready-to-wear) at that time. The accessories shown highlight new trends and give you ideas for a total fashion concept.

If a pattern has variations in the neckline, sleeve or hem length, each option is shown in a different view. Usually each view is marked by a letter, which correlates to the yardage (metrage) and notions information listed, by view, on the pattern envelope back.

The pattern envelope front also includes the style number and size. When the pattern is created by a European or an American fashion designer, his or her name also appears on the envelope front.

To make shopping easier, vertically circle your size and all yardage (metrage) information on the pattern envelope so you won't waste time hunting for it over and over again. Underline the amount of fabric you need for the fabric width you have. Circle or underline all the notions, trims and interfacings you need for the view you are making, for your size.

To facilitate wardrobe-building, staple or tape swatches of garments you're matching or coordinating right to the pattern envelope so you can visualize style, color and texture on the spot.

Very Easy Vogue

PATTERN/PATRON
SIZE/TAILLE

PATTERN ENVELOPE BACK

The envelope back, in addition to providing all the detail, fabric and notion information you need for making your purchases, is printed both in English and French and in Imperial and metric measurements to meet certain packaging laws and to make the envelopes functional in French-speaking Canada and parts of Europe, also. Usually the French and metric information is listed separately from the English and Imperial information, to keep confusion to a minimum.

The **garment description** is a succinct explanation of each garment piece, including details that may not be visible on the illustration or photograph on the envelope front, such as concealed pockets or side zippers. The size and garment category—"Misses' dress," for example—prefaces the rest of the descriptive copy. The description includes fitting terms, such as "very loose-fitting," to help you understand how the designer intended the garment to relate to the body. Other special information, such as "purchased belts," is listed here, too.

It is important to read this description—thoroughly—before purchasing a pattern, for a complete understanding of what the finished garment should look like and to anticipate how it will fit you.

If you often re-use your patterns, note any changes you've made such as "lengthen jacket and sleeves 2" (5cm), need extra 1/8 yd. (.15m)," right on the envelope as a fabric buying guide for next time. It's easy to forget what you've done from one project to another.

Back views and, if space permits, front views are fine, technical drawings that show all construction and styling details very clearly.

Notions are listed separately, to serve as your buying guide for all the items other than fabric, lining, underlining or interfacing that you need to complete your garment. Recommended sizes are included, such as 16" (40cm) zipper.

Fabric recommendations listed are those fabric types most suited to the design, as determined by the designer. Often the list is preceded by fabric category suggestions, such as "soft" or "crisp," to give you a further guideline as to the intended overall look of the garment when it is constructed.

Fabric suitability information often is included with fabric recommendations. This tells you such things as whether the design is unsuitable for obvious diagonal fabrics, stripes, plaids or napped fabrics. If the pattern *is* suitable, there is a statement that reads "allow extra fabric to match plaids or stripes." How much extra is something the pattern companies can't tell you, since print sizes and shapes vary from fabric to fabric, requiring more or less extra for matching.

The abbreviations "w/wo" indicate whether the yardage

SAMPLE ENVELOPE BACK

$8.50
CAN. $4.50
AUST. *$5.00
N.Z. *$5.50

*suggested price
*prix suggeré

DEVANT A
FRONT A

DEVANT B
FRONT B

Back Views

Garment Description — MISSES' DRESS. Loose-fitting, straight dress, below mid-knee, has extended shoulders, shoulder pads, side front seams, inside ties, flaps, side pockets and short or long sleeves. B: roll collar. Purchased belt.

Notions — NOTIONS: ½" (13mm) Covered Shoulder Pads or Vogue #8817, Eight ¾" (20mm) Buttons, Snaps and Seam Binding.

Fabric Recommendation — FABRICS: Ltwt. Gabardine, Ltwt. Flannel, Serge, Linen, Silk Broadcloth and Chambray. Unsuitable for obvious diagonals. Allow extra fabric to match plaids or stripes. Use nap yardages/layouts for pile, shaded or one-way design fabrics.   * with nap.   ** w/o nap.

ROBE. Robe au-dessous du genou, droite et ample, à panneau devant, rabats fausses-poches, attaches intérieures, poches dans les coutures, épaules rembourrées et manches montées bas, courtes ou longues. Col roulé pour B. Ceinture fantaisie.

MERCERIE - Epaulettes recouvertes (13mm) ou faites avec le patron Vogue 8817 - 8 boutons (20mm) - Boutons-pression - Ruban bordure.

TISSUS - Gabardine ou flanelle légères - Serge - Lin - Popeline de soie - Chambray. Les grandes diagonales ne conviennent pas. Compte non tenu des raccords de rayures ou carreaux. * avec sens (tissu pelucheux, à reflet ou certains imprimés)   ** sans sens.

Size Range / **Yardage Block**

8	10	12	14	16	18	SIZE/TAILLE	8	10	12	14	16	18
DRESS A							ROBE A					
3⅜	3⅜	3⅜	3½	3½	4⅜	35"(90cm)*/**	3.10	3.10	3.10	3.20	3.20	4.00
2¾	2¾	3⅛	3⅛	3⅛	3½	45"(115cm)*/**	2.60	2.60	2.90	2.90	2.90	3.20
2⅜	2⅝	2⅝	2¾	2¾	2¾	60"(150cm)*/**	2.20	2.40	2.40	2.60	2.60	2.60
DRESS B							ROBE B					
3⅞	4	4¼	4¼	4⅜	4⅞	35"(90cm)*/**	3.60	3.70	3.90	3.90	4.00	4.50
2⅞	2⅞	3½	3½	3⅝	3¾	45"(115cm)*/**	3.20	3.20	3.20	3.20	3.40	3.50
2⅜	2¾	2¾	2¾	2¾	2¾	60"(150cm)*/**	2.20	2.60	2.60	2.60	2.60	2.60
INTERFACING A OR B (Fusible)							ENTOILAGE A ou B (Thermocollant)					
1⅜	1⅜	1⅜	1⅜	1½	1½	18,24"(46,61cm)	1.30	1.30	1.30	1.30	1.40	1.40
LINING A OR B (Pockets)							DOUBLURE A ou B (Poches)					
½	½	½	½	½	½	45"(115cm)	0.50	0.50	0.50	0.50	0.50	0.50

Finished Garment Measurements

						WIDTHS/LARGEURS Dress/Robe			à l'ourlet (croisé non compris)			
Lower edge (excl. overlap)												
39	40	41½	43½	45½	47½	.... A,B	99	102	105	110	116	121

						LENGTHS/LONGUEURS Dress/Robe				nuque à ourlet		
Finished back from base of neck												
41½	41¾	42	42¼	42½	42¾	.... A,B	105	106	107	107	108	109

(metrage) listed is for fabrics with (w) or without (wo) nap. This refers to how the pattern pieces are laid out on the fabric. It is important to realize that the word "nap" in this instance refers not only to napped or pile fabrics such as corduroy or velvet, but also to fabrics that show shading, such as satin and knits. "Nap" also refers to any printed fabric that has a definite top and bottom. For example, a floral print that is not scattered but has one-directional stems you would like to have pointing to the hem must be cut using a with-nap layout. If it isn't, your garment back could have stems pointing toward your shoulder while the front has them properly "planted"!

Layouts for fabrics *with* nap have all pattern pieces placed in the same direction, from the top of the garment to the bottom. Layouts for fabrics *without* nap may have pattern pieces placed in either direction. If the indication is "without nap only," and you have a napped, shaded or directional fabric, you may have to purchase extra to accommodate a "with nap" layout.

The **size range** is the sequence of numbers that indicates in which sizes the pattern is available. Each size really becomes a column heading for yardage (metrage) requirements.

The **yardage (metric) block** gives the yardage (metrage) requirements for each garment, style or view, usually in several fabric widths. The amount of fabric needed is listed next to the fabric widths.

The widths shown correlate to the fabric recommendations and are carefully measured and checked to be as economical as possible for you. Unless you know you need to match a fabric pattern or add extra inches to the width or length of the finished garment, there is no need to buy more than the required amount.

Finished garment measurements are the width at the lower edge—which gives you the hem circumference of the garment—and the finished back length. The width at lower edge measurement helps you understand how narrow or full the silhouette is. If you know the finished garment length you need or prefer for your body type, comparing your measurements with this measurement gives you a handy reference for any pattern tissue length adjustments you may need to make.

Fitted, close fitting, loose fitting, semi fitted, very loose fitting . . . these are the terms you'll find used consistently in the garment descriptions on pattern envelopes. The chart below lists Vogue's standards for fit, and the terms tell you exactly what to anticipate when it comes to fitting. Each term indicates a general amount of wearing ease and design ease that is built into the pattern. Ease is the amount of "space" in a garment beyond the body measurements. This chart indicates the amount of ease allowed for silhouettes used in garment descriptions. Ease allowances are given in ranges from the minimum to the maximum amount allowed for each silhouette; the specific amount of ease varies from style to style.

EASE CHART*

Silhouette	BUST AREA			HIP AREA
	DRESSES, BLOUSES, SHIRTS, TOPS, VESTS	JACKETS Lined or Unlined	COATS Lined or Unlined	SKIRTS, PANTS, SHORTS, CULOTTES
Close fitting	0-2⅞" (0-7.3cm)	not applicable		not applicable
Fitted	3-4" (7.5-10cm)	3¾-4¼" (9.5-10.7cm)	5¼-6¾" (13.3-17cm)	2-3" (5-7.5cm)
Semi-fitted	4⅛-5" (10.4-12.5cm)	4⅜-5¾" (11.1-14.5cm)	6⅞-8" (17.4-20.5cm)	3⅛-4" (7.9-10cm)
Loose fitting	5⅛-8" (13-20.5cm)	5⅞-10" (14.8-25.5cm)	8⅛-12" (20.7-30.5cm)	4⅛-6" (10.4-15cm)
Very loose fitting	over 8" (over 20.5cm)	over 10" (over 25.5cm)	over 12" (over 30.5cm)	over 6 " (over 15cm)

Ease allowances given are not applicable for garments designed for stretchable knit fabrics

How to Lay Out a Pattern

An important part of laying out a pattern is preparation. The extra time it takes to get everything ready actually saves time, later. If you are careful about grainline, cutting exactly on the cutting line and preparing your fabric and pattern tissue, odds are you'll achieve a garment that drapes and fits the way it should. You will avoid spending a lot of time trying to correct errors that often are uncorrectable. A cutting line error of just 1/4" (6mm) around a pattern piece can be multiplied to 1" (25mm) when two seams are affected. This inaccuracy could mean wasting time ripping out and restitching seams. Precision and accuracy at this point make what follows not only easy sewing but pleasurable sewing, as well.

PREPARING YOUR FABRIC

How do you know which is the right side of your fabric? Sometimes, if the print, color and texture are the same on both sides, it doesn't matter. But sometimes it does matter, and there are a few guidelines that will help you determine which is the right side. One indication is the way the fabric is folded when you buy it. Cottons and linens are folded right side out on the bolt, while wools are folded wrong side out. If a fabric is rolled on a tube, it is rolled with the right side to the inside.

If you've already washed or refolded your fabric, the surface or texture gives you a clue. Textured fabrics usually are more defined on the right side, and smooth fabrics are slicker, shinier or softer on the right side.

Printed fabrics are more distinct on the right side, slightly fuzzy or blurred on the wrong side.

The first step in preparing your fabric is to preshrink it according to the care instructions. You can do this by simply washing the fabric along with your regular clothes. Then press it to eliminate wrinkles and the center crease line. For fabrics that must be dry cleaned, have them professionally dry cleaned or steam them using a press cloth and steam iron.

After preshrinking, look at the fabric carefully to determine the grainlines. Understanding how the fabric is constructed and the direction of each grainline helps you in laying out your pattern.

Woven fabrics have fixed yarns that go in the lengthwise direction. Along the lengthwise edge is a firmly woven strip, or selvage. The selvage is always indicated in the fabric cutting layout. The lengthwise grain, or straight grain, has very little stretch or give and generally is the top-to-bottom direction for your garment.

At right angles to the lengthwise yarns are the crosswise yarns. The crosswise grain has more stretch or give to it, and usually is the side-to-side direction of your garment.

A diagonal that intersects the two grainlines is called the bias. True bias is at a 45° angle to any straight edge when the lengthwise and crosswise grains are perpendicular. Bias stretches the most and gives the softest drape to a finished garment.

When the lengthwise and crosswise grains are at right angles to each other, the fabric is on-grain. However, the yarns can be pulled out of alignment during the manufacturing process. If this happens, you must re-align them to place your grainlines at perfect right angles.

A fabric which is off-grain should be straightened so that your finished garment hangs correctly. Fabrics with finishes, such as permanent press, water repellent, etc., cannot be straightened. Also, a fabric that is printed off-grain cannot be corrected. Check print fabrics carefully. If the design seems crooked, even if the grainlines are straight, don't buy them.

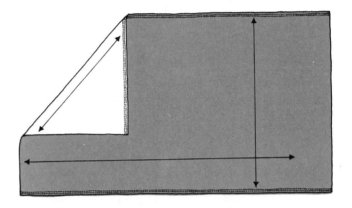

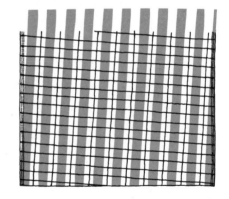

OFF-GRAIN FABRIC

49

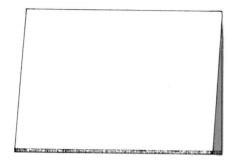

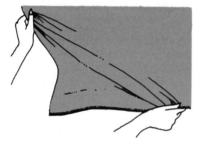

Straighten the fabric ends by pulling a thread across one crosswise end. To do this, snip the selvage on one side and gently pull one or two threads (as you would a gathering thread) until you reach the opposite selvage. This gives you a perfectly straight cutting line in the crosswise direction. Cut along the pulled thread.

Now fold the fabric lengthwise bringing the selvages together and the crosswise ends together. If the fabric doesn't align on three sides or if the corners don't form right angles, then it is off-grain and needs to be straightened.

To straighten, pull the fabric very gently, but firmly, on the bias until the corners form right angles naturally. Don't use brute force, however, or you could stretch your fabric completely out of shape.

Knit fabrics are formed of interlocking loops of yarn that are called ribs. These ribs are comparable to the lengthwise direction of a woven fabric. Other loops are at right angles to the ribs, and are like the crosswise grain of a woven fabric.

If the right and wrong sides of your fabric are not obvious, mark the wrong side with tape, chalk, thread or a small safety pin so you can easily identify it. Mark all layers of each piece, too, after you've cut out your pattern, to avoid confusion as you sew.

Course

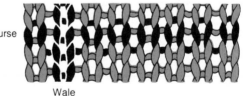

Wale

PREPARING YOUR PATTERN

Pattern companies generally fold tissue by machine and then tightly compress the envelopes to eliminate air pockets and make the folds and the tissue compact and flat. That's great for packaging, but can cause creased tissue. If you can't smooth the tissue flat with your hands, press it with a warm, dry, iron . . . creases and wrinkles in pattern pieces can distort measurements.

Pattern pieces are named and/or numbered, so it's easy to pull out the pieces you need for the garment you are making. Return the ones you won't be using to the envelope to avoid confusion.

Often small pieces, such as for pockets and interfacings, are printed on one sheet. Cut them apart, but *not* on the cutting line. Leave the extra tissue around all pattern pieces to use for alterations, if necessary.

Read the tissue as carefully as you read the envelope. Each piece is printed with the number of times and how it is to be cut. You may need two backs or two pockets, for example, or the front is to be placed on a fold, not cut on all sides. Knowing this information before you begin helps you understand and follow the cutting guide more readily.

If you need to lengthen or shorten the pattern, be sure to check that you have done so on all corresponding pattern pieces . . . all is lost if you lengthen the bodice front but not the back or facings!

If you re-use your patterns frequently, keep them from becoming dog-eared and fragile by bonding them to fusible interfacing or to the plastic-coated side of freezer paper.

SELECTING THE CORRECT LAYOUT

Pattern instruction sheets are organized in a step-by-step format. Once again, do a little reading before you put pins to paper and fabric, so you have a grasp of how each piece is going to be joined to the next. Read the instruction sheet through once, then go back to the first section, which is the fabric cutting layout.

To find the correct layout, look for the one that corresponds to your garment view, size and fabric width. There may be several layouts for the garment you are making if the pattern is measured for different fabric widths and if there are with- and without-nap guides. Each has been designed for the most economical use of your fabric, and each has a different arrangement. For example, a fabric that is 60″ (150cm) wide has a shorter, wider layout than one that is 35″ (90cm) because there is more room to lay pieces side by side. A narrower fabric has a layout with more pieces end to end. The selvages and fold always are indicated. Placing your fabric in the same direction makes it easier to follow the layout.

The cutting layout on the instruction sheet shows fabric folded right sides together for a double thickness and right side up for a single thickness.

Every instruction sheet includes a key for the various symbols used on the cutting layout. For example, a shaded pattern piece is to be placed

SELVAGES

←⟶ 12 ⟶

13

SELVAGES

✱ See SPECIAL INSTRUCTIONS

with the printed or right side of the tissue facing the fabric and a white pattern piece is to be placed with the printed side facing up. Read and understand this guide before proceeding.

If there are special cutting instructions, there will be an indication on a particular piece or an entire layout.

For instance, a pattern piece which has a star on it, or the words "right side up" next to it, is to be cut only once with the printed side up on the right side of a single layer of fabric.

An asterisk close to a layout points out special instructions for preparing the fabric before cutting. The fabric must first be folded in half on the crosswise grain with right sides together. Then it is cut apart along the fold. Keeping the right sides together, turn the upper layer around so that the nap, shading or one-way design runs in the same direction.

Always lay out the entire pattern before cutting, to make sure you have enough fabric.

If your fabric is slippery or tends to shift a little, pin the selvages together every few inches, after you fold the fabric for layout, so everything lines up perfectly.

To keep slippery fabrics from sliding when you're laying them out, put a flannel- or fabric-backed plastic cloth on your cutting board or table, fabric side up.

Once you have determined which cutting guide to follow, circle it so your eye can find it fast as you work.

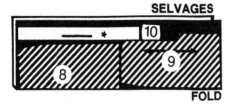

SELVAGES

FOLD

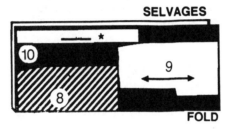

SELVAGES

FOLD

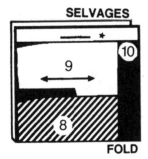

SELVAGES

FOLD

Fabrics can have definite odors caused by chemicals used in processing. You may sneeze or find your eyes watering as you work with them. Wash these fabrics before you start, and add a cup of baking soda to remove odors.

Save a "getting ready" step and preshrink fabrics as you press instead of in the washer. Use a steam iron and plenty of steam.

PINNING AND CUTTING

The first pinning procedure to follow is to align and pin the grainline arrow printed on the pattern tissue. It should be pinned parallel to the selvage edge on a woven fabric and parallel to the fold on a knit fabric. Pin one arrow tip and measure from the arrow to the selvage. Now measure from the other end of the arrow to the selvage, adjusting until the second measurement is equal to the first. When you use this method, your pattern cannot shift off-grain.

A pattern piece that is to be placed on a fold should be pinned on the fold first, with the tissue foldline precisely at the edge of the fabric fold. Smooth the tissue as you continue to pin, corners first, then edges.

The fastest and most efficient way to place pins is diagonally at corners and perpendicular to the edges, with the points toward the cutting line. Fabrics in which pins could leave holes should be pinned within the seam allowance only.

Always keep the fabric flat on the cutting surface. Never let your fabric hang over your cutting surface while pinning or cutting, as the weight of the fabric can pull and distort, undoing all your careful measuring, straightening and aligning. Bent-handled shears help you keep the fabric flat as you cut, which is important for accuracy. If you pick fabric up to cut it, it's very easy to cut in too far or to veer off the cutting line. Make firm, long cuts, sliding the shears along to make the next cut while holding your other hand flat on the pattern piece, near the cutting line, for the smoothest edge. This gives you good control and helps keep the pattern and fabric from slipping. Because it is possible to cut too far with the tips of your shears, cut notches outside the cutting line, not into it.

Save cutting time on pattern pieces with a straight edge that are laid out on the straight grain by placing the cutting lines directly on the selvage. This gives you an already-finished seam that won't ravel. Clip the selvage every few inches to prevent puckering and pulling.

For double or triple notches, cut straight across from point to point instead of cutting each notch individually. This is faster than cutting around each little triangle and easy to spot when you're joining seams.

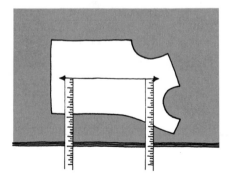

How to Mark
Your Fabric

It cannot be stressed too many times that accurate marking makes sewing easier and faster. If you've always thought of marking as your number-one drudge sewing task, you probably have not experimented with alternative methods. Most people use only one marking system for all fabrics, because it was the one they were taught when they learned to sew. If that describes you, too, do a little experimenting and discover how much easier marking your fabric can be with different tools and methods. See page 24 for a review of marking tools.

WHEN AND WHERE TO MARK

All the pattern symbols, which are your sewing road map for step-by-step garment construction, should be transferred to your fabric after each pattern piece is cut out, but before the pattern tissue is removed. These symbols can vary among the different pattern companies, but the instruction sheet defines what they are. Large solid circles ●, small solid circles •, squares ■, and triangles ▲ are examples of symbols that need to be transferred. In addition to these symbols, darts (A), placement lines (B), tuck or pleat lines (C) and button and buttonhole markings should be marked. The notches along the cutting lines are another kind of symbol, which you "mark" when you cut and do not need to mark again.

Do not take the time to mark stitching lines; simply line up your fabric edge with the guide on your sewing machine base or a piece of tape placed at the correct measurement for stitching. Do, however, mark seamlines on curves and other places where your machine seam guide would be covered or difficult to see during stitching. If there are other lines that you are not sure whether to mark, go ahead and mark them. This saves you the time it would take to re-pin the pattern tissue and mark later if you discover you need the marking after all.

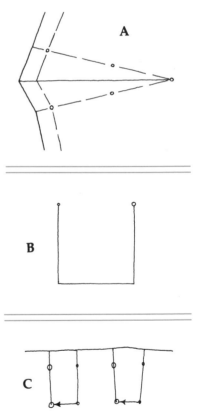

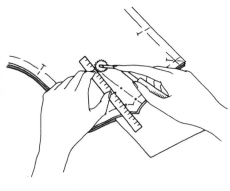

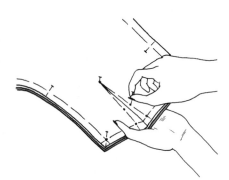

TRACING PAPER AND TRACING WHEEL

A tracing wheel and tracing paper are easy and fast to use for marking firmly woven or knitted fabrics. Markings should always be transferred to the *wrong* side of your fabric, since they can be permanent. Pre-test on a scrap of your fabric. Don't use this method on even the wrong side of sheer fabrics, because marks may show through.

To mark one layer of fabric, place a sheet of tracing paper between the pattern and the fabric, carbon side against the *wrong* side of your fabric. Press firmly on the tracing wheel and trace the markings on your pattern tissue. Use a ruler or other straight edge to guide the wheel. Mark an "X" on dots, squares, dart points and other small pattern markings. To mark two layers of fabric at a time, which are pinned right sides together, fold one sheet of single-faced tracing paper in half, carbon side in, and insert it around the fabric layers.

PINS AND TAILOR'S CHALK

Test tailor's chalk on your fabric before using this method, to make sure the chalk marks will be visible and that they can be removed. Also test pins on your fabric. If the pins you normally use leave holes or cause runs, try a finer silk pin. If that also leaves marks, don't use this marking method.

To mark, first push pins straight down through the tissue marking point and layers of fabric. Holding the tissue in place, pull the tissue off *over* the marking pins, leaving them in the fabric. Make a chalk mark at each pin on the wrong side of each fabric layer. Remove the pins and, using a ruler, connect the chalk marks at darts and other places where you need a continuous line for a stitching guide.

MARKING PENS AND PENCILS

Fabric marking pens and pencils are used with pins in the same manner as is tailor's chalk. When you no longer need the markings, marks from pencils can be brushed off and marks from pens either are removed with water or disappear in 24 to 48 hours. Both may be used on the right side of your fabric, but, as with any other marking method, pre-test on a fabric scrap to make sure the marks aren't indelible.

When you use a tracing wheel and tracing paper, the pattern tissue can tear. If you plan to re-use your pattern, first put transparent nonyellowing tape over all the symbols to keep them intact for future use.

How to Baste

Basting, which is the method of holding garment pieces in place before stitching, has come a long way since the days when it was done only by hand. New inventions and aids, combined with shortcuts, have made basting a much faster procedure. Never skip this step. It is very time-consuming to rip out machine stitches because a fabric slipped or shifted during stitching—something that doesn't happen if you take a little time to baste first.

PIN BASTING

Match all pattern markings on your garment pieces and place pins, perpendicular to the seamline, 1" to 4" (25mm to 10cm) apart. Place pins closer together when fabrics are slippery or hard to handle and at curves and corners, where you will be pivoting or turning the fabric during stitching. For straight seam stitching on easy-to-handle fabrics, pins may be placed farther apart.

Begin stitching, slowing down as you get to each pin.

Remove the pins as you reach them, because sewing over them can break or chip sewing machine needles.

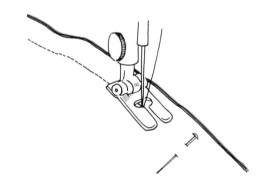

MACHINE BASTING

To machine baste, you have to pin baste first, to hold fabric edges in place. Machine basting is a much faster method than hand basting and is very useful when you want to check fit before machine stitching. Set your machine to its longest stitch length and stitch, removing pins as you reach them. Clip the stitches about every inch (25mm) for easy removal of basting threads when you finish stitching. Pull basting threads out as soon as you have machine-stitched so they won't get caught in other stitching and become difficult to remove.

BASTING TAPE

Basting tape is a fast aid for general basting usage and is a real plus for hard-to-handle fabrics that may pucker or slip out of pins. Place the tape 1/4" (6mm) from the stitching line, in the seam allowance, so it won't be caught in the stitching. Stitching over basting tape makes it almost impossible to remove completely. As with basting threads, remove it as soon as you have finished machine-stitching so it won't get caught in other seams or stitches.

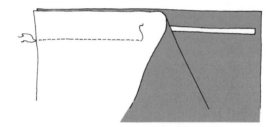

DISAPPEARING BASTING TAPE

A new basting aid, borrowed from the medical profession where its prototype has been used in surgical procedures, is double-sided disappearing basting tape. It is used like regular basting tape, but, because it dissolves and disappears when your garment is washed, you can stitch through it and don't have to remove it after stitching. Do not press over it, however, until you have washed the garment.

It is applied about 1/16" (2mm) from the stitching line on one layer of fabric. Remove the backing and finger-press the second layer of fabric in place.

GLUE STICK BASTING

A glue stick, like basting tape, provides a very fast way to hold seams, trims, pockets, facings or zippers in place before stitching. It works best on firmly woven or knitted fabrics that don't slip or ripple.

Simply roll it along the sections to be basted and press them together with your fingers. Although glue sticks are manufactured to wash out completely, test your fabric before you glue garment sections.

NO BASTING

If you're at the point of super-speed sewing and want to skip the basting step, it is possible, with many easy-sew fabrics, to align the top edges and the matching marks on your fabric and stitch without basting.

Guide the fabric under the pressure foot with your left hand behind it and your right hand in front, keeping the two layers even at the edges. This is not a good method for slippery fabrics or on seams where a lot of easing is required.

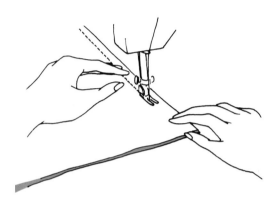

HAND BASTING

Because it is a slower method than the other basting techniques, use hand basting to hold your fabric in place only for areas that require a great deal of easing or for sharp corners and curves that might not align perfectly with other basting methods. For a general guideline, keep your stitches about 1" (25mm) apart and make each stitch about 1/2" (13mm) long, but don't worry about measuring them accurately. Make them a little shorter when you need more control.

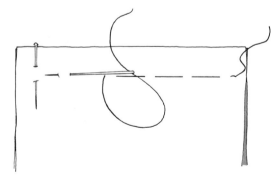

How to Press

When people ask you if you made what you're wearing, it should be because it's so exquisitely beautiful that you couldn't possibly have found it in a store . . . not because the seams aren't flat or the corners are indented or the sleeve caps are creased. If they're asking you for the wrong reasons, then you may be doing one of two things incorrectly. Either you are not pressing as you sew or you are ironing instead of pressing.

Remember, part of the art of easy sewing is making your ironing board, iron and pressing tools an integral part of your sewing area so you easily can press every step of the way. If you wait until your garment is completed to press, it is too late to achieve the curves, contours and smooth edges that are part of its built-in design.

Ironing is sliding or pushing the iron across your garment sections in a back-and-forth direction. Ironing before your garment is completed can cause wrinkles and distort the fabric, and it prevents you from accomplishing fine shaping and sculpturing. *Pressing* is moving your iron up and down, not back and forth. When this motion is used in combination with pressing aids and tools, the result is beautiful shaping and beautiful garments. See pages 35–37 for a review of pressing tools.

There are a few basic rules that apply whenever you press.

- *Always press-test a scrap of your fabric first to determine the correct heat setting. Too hot an iron could cause sticking, puckering, smoking or even melting, and too cool an iron won't be effective. Also check the way your fabric reacts to steam and moisture. If it reacts badly it could pucker, become dulled, or show water or scorch marks.*

- *Press on the wrong side of your fabric whenever you can. If you have no alternative but to press on the right side, always use a pressing cloth to avoid marks and shiny spots.*

- *Press with the grain of the fabric to avoid crosswise or bias stretching or pulling.*

- *Never press over pins or basting thread. They can leave impressions and mar your fabric, and pins can scratch the bottom of your iron.*

- *Press darts and seams before other stitching crosses them, to prevent bulk and a bunchy appearance on the right side of the garment.*

- *Use steam, if your fabric tests well, to achieve flat seams, sharp edges and creases and soft rolls and curves. Hold the iron about 3" (7.5cm) from your fabric for shaping, press the steam button and mold the garment section while it is damp. To apply the iron directly, use a press cloth between it and your fabric and lift the iron up and down. Allow your fabric to dry thoroughly before continuing to the next construction step.*

- *Cut brown paper bags into strips. When pressing, place them between the darts, pleats or seam allowances and your garment to keep the darts, pleats, or seam allowances from leaving impressions on the right side of your fabric. The strips should be at least 2" (5cm) wider than the area to be pressed, so that you don't press over their edges, which also could leave impressions.*

- *Before you press sharp creases or pressed pleats, check the fit of your garment. It can be very difficult to press creases out of some fabrics if you have to make an adjustment.*

Substitute wide strips torn from a canvas pressing cloth for brown paper to use when pressing darts, pleats and seams. If you dampen them when you use them, you don't need to use steam. Keep them rolled, with your pressing tools, to use each time you sew.

A soleplate attachment enables you to press on the right side of your fabric without a pressing cloth, giving you greater visibility. For easy maintenance, a non-stick soleplate will not become coated with any residue from fusible materials.

PRESSING DARTS

Because darts give fit and curve to your garment, they should be pressed on a curved surface, such as a tailor's ham or press mitt, rather than on a flat surface.

First, press only the dart, the way it was stitched, just to its point. Then, with the garment section open, press it in the direction indicated on your instruction sheet. Usually horizontal darts are pressed downward and vertical darts are pressed toward the center front or back. Press from the wide end toward the point.

If a dart is slashed open, press with the tip of your iron and a press cloth, opening the edges and pressing toward the dart point.

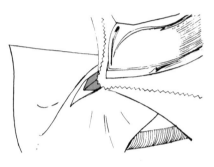

PRESSING GATHERS

Garment areas that have been gathered need to be handled carefully so that you do not press in wrinkles or sharp creases. Hold the garment section at the stitching and press from below the gathers toward the stitching. When you reach the beginning of the gathers, use the tip of the iron to press between the fabric folds.

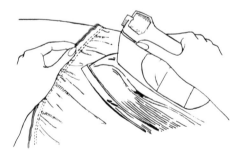

If you need to create clouds of steam, a length of aluminum foil placed under your ironing board cover will help by retaining and bouncing back moisture before it has a chance to evaporate.

If your iron's soleplate needs cleaning, use commercial cleaning solution, which is widely available.

If you need to remove a crease, spray it with a solution of equal parts white vinegar and water, and press over a pressing cloth. If that doesn't work, spray white vinegar alone. Pre-test on a scrap of fabric to be sure your garment can tolerate vinegar.

PRESSING HEMS

Steaming and pressing hems before they are finished makes the finishing a lot easier, especially when there is extra fullness at the raw edge, which must be eased as you hem. Place brown paper between the hem and the garment to prevent marks, then steam and press lightly without pressing over pins or basting thread. This method shrinks some of the fullness, giving you less to have to ease. When you have sewn the hem, steam again, pressing if you want a crisp edge.

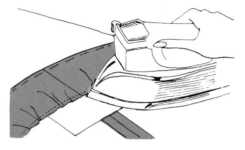

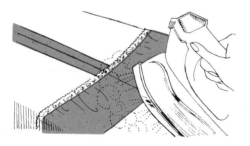

PRESSING PLEATS

Taking the time to press pleats as they are constructed prevents pleats that droop or hang incorrectly and ensures perfect alignment with the rest of your garment.

Crisp Pleats

Once pleats are basted, press both the right and the wrong side just enough to set the pleats without permanently creasing them. To prevent marks or crease impressions from showing on the fabric under the pleat, place strips of brown bag paper under the pleat folds before you press. Use a press cloth and a small amount of steam. If the pleats hang correctly when you try on the garment, press again to within 8" (20.5cm) of the lower edge, using steam and a press cloth to set them permanently. After hemming, press the creases in the lower edges of the pleats.

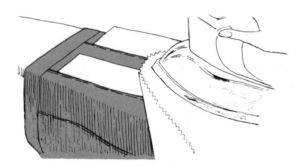

Soft Pleats

Soft pleats are steam-set rather than pressed. Pin the pleats in place on your ironing board cover. Hold the iron 2" to 3" (5–7.5cm) from the pleats and steam them. Allow the fabric to dry thoroughly before removing it from the ironing board.

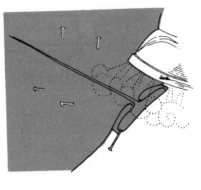

Hemline Pleats

Hemline pleats that fold on a seam line often protrude or don't fall in place properly. This can be corrected by careful pressing before hemming. First, clip the pleat seam right at the top of the turned-up hem and, if it's not already done, press open the seam allowance below the clip. Trim the seam allowance in the hem. Then press a sharp crease in the underfold, using a press cloth and steam. If the fold still protrudes, stitch close to the edge and press again.

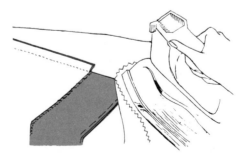

PRESSING SEAMS

All seams, like darts, are first pressed flat along the stitching line in the same direction as the seam was stitched. Then the seams are pressed open, according to their contours.

Flat Seams

Use a seam roll under flat seams or place strips of brown paper between the seam allowances and the garment to keep ridges from forming on the right side of your garment. Open the seam with the tip of your iron and use steam, if your fabric reacts well to it, as you press, protecting your fabric with a press cloth.

Curved Seams

A curved seam should be pressed open, but it should not have its natural contours pressed out. To maintain the shape, use a tailor's ham or a press mitt as your pressing surface. Use brown paper under the seam allowances and a press cloth between the seam and your iron.

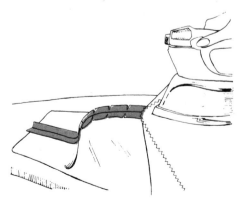

Enclosed Seams

When the seam allowances are enclosed during construction, they should be pressed before they are turned. These kinds of seams are found on facings, cuffs, some collars and pocket flaps. Because these seam areas often are small, put them over the edge of a point presser for easy pressing access, and open and press them with the tip of the iron. Pressing the seam open makes turning to the right side easier and gives a defined edge that won't shift or roll.

Next, place the seam area flat with the underside up and turn the seam allowances to the wrong side until you can just see the stitching line. Press lightly in place. This, again, keeps the seam from rolling when you turn the section right side out.

Now turn the section right side out. As you press, make sure the seam stays on the underside. Do not press the seam toward the side of the garment section that will show when garment construction is completed. Use a press cloth during this final pressing, to protect the fabric.

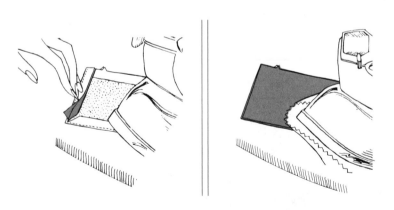

PRESSING SLEEVES

If set-in sleeves are your particular sewing dislike, read the easy sewing techniques for constructing them on page 170 after you read this. If you are *not* using flat construction methods to sew set-in sleeves, use these pressing techniques to set in a sleeve easily and perfectly, and all those mysterious extra tucks, wrinkles and creases will disappear from your sleeve-sewing projects forever.

Use a sleeve board and iron to press the sleeve seam open. If you don't have access to a sleeve board, use a seam roll instead.

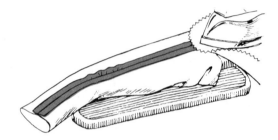

When you have eased and fitted the sleeve cap by adjusting the gathering threads, remove the sleeve from your garment. To maintain the shape of the sleeve cap, work on the right side of the sleeve cap, pressing it over the curved surface of a press mitt. Use only the tip and edges of your iron, with steam, to shrink the extra fullness from *just* the seam allowance.

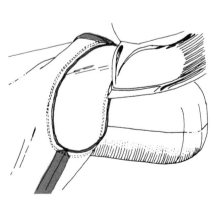

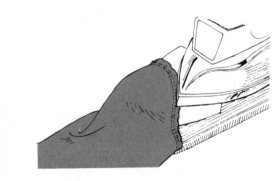

To press the finished sleeve, after you have stitched it into your garment, place it over a tailor's ham and press along the seam, using very little steam and avoiding the sleeve cap so you don't press in unnecessary creases.

FINISHED PRESSING

All these special pressing points apply to other garment areas that you need to press as you sew, such as plackets, tucks and zippers. Use the same pressing principles, letting the shape of the garment area determine which pressing aids and tools you use. The final pressing you give your completed garment should be only a light one, to smooth and remove any surface wrinkles that may have formed during finishing. Any area that needs a little steam to set it may be padded with tissue paper to hold the shape while the fabric dries. When you send a suit to the dry cleaner, it often is returned to you with tissue paper at the sleeve cap, under the collar or in the sleeves for the same purpose, as well as to keep these curved areas from being crushed.

How to Use Fusible Interfacing

Many areas of a garment need to be stabilized with interfacing, which is available in two types, fusible and non-fusible. The interfacing recommended in this book is fusible only, since it is faster and easier to apply.

Fusible interfacings are fabrics which are coated on one side with a heat-sensitive bonding agent. When you press these fabrics, using a combination of heat and steam, the bonding agent melts and fuses the interfacing to your garment section. Usually, this is a one-step procedure with your iron replacing the hand and machine sewing steps needed with non-fusible interfacings.

Although fusible interfacing is a great timesaver, be sure to take the time to test it on your fabric to make sure it gives your garment sections the appearance, crispness or softness you desire. In general, the bonding agent tends to add extra body to the garment fabric and slightly changes its character. Not all fabrics are suitable for fusibles, especially very sheer fabrics, acetates and those that are treated with silicone.

There are a multitude of fusible interfacing products available. They come in different weights, fibers and colors and may be either woven or non-woven. Each kind has its own instructions, which do vary from type to type and from manufacturer to manufacturer, so be sure to request directions when you make your purchase, and be sure to follow them to the letter—imperfectly bonded interfacing blisters and pulls away from the fabric during washing or dry cleaning and cannot be re-bonded.

Fusible interfacings are sold both by the yard (or meter) and in pre-cut packages for specific garment areas, such as waistbands, straight facings, shirt plackets and cuffs.

Your choice of interfacing depends on the fashion fabric you've selected. Your fabric and interfacing should be compatible in care requirements, weight, color and hand, the technical term for the feel of a fabric. In general, interfacing should be slightly lighter weight than your fabric. Select a color that blends with the fabric—use dark interfacings with dark colors and white or beige interfacings with white or light colors.

Take into consideration the hand of the fashion fabric and the design of your pattern—firm, crisp fabrics or design details need crisp interfacings; soft, drapable fabrics or designs require lighter, softer interfacings. Test by laying the interfacing over your fashion fabric to check color, then feel the two layers together to test weight and hand. Remember, a fusible interfacing fuses directly to your fabric. This process causes the fabric to have a slightly heavier, firmer appearance.

The chart which follows is a reference for the interfacings recommended for different fabric weights. Use it when planning your purchases for sewing projects. Use the following general guidelines as you construct your garment, in conjunction with the specific fusible interfacing instructions from the companies that manufacture them.

- *To lay out lightweight or sheer fusible interfacings, place the interfacing fabric over the pattern piece and trace just outside the seamline into the seam allowance. Remove the interfacing and cut the pieces out just along the traced line. Cut any corners, diagonally, to remove bulk.*

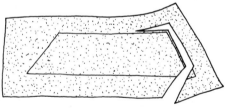

- *Always use a damp press cloth during fusing. It helps create steam and protects the soleplate of your iron from fusing resins.*

- *Once fusible interfacing pieces are cut out, fuse them directly to the facing, not to the garment. This method makes positioning easy, since the interfacing usually is identical to the facing, and prevents the possibility of the outline of the interfacing showing on the outside of the garment. Interfacing should be applied to the upper collar and the outside of waistbands or cuffs.*

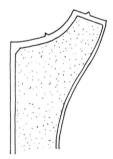

71

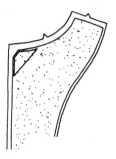

• If your garment needs extra body in an area that is already interfaced, you may fuse a second layer of interfacing on top of the first. This can be done for an entire waistband or belt, or in smaller areas, such as the point of a lapel.

• If the buttonhole area of the garment has not been interfaced, reinforce the buttonholes by fusing a small piece of interfacing to the fabric before you stitch. Pink the edges so there won't be a defined straight line showing on the right side of the fabric. Use a dark color interfacing for dark fabric and a light one for fabric with a light ground, so that when the buttonhole is cut open, contrasting threads aren't a problem.

• If you feel you need to baste your interfacing in place before fusing, first pin it and then steam baste with the tip of your iron, pressing lightly at a few points around the edges. Remove the pins. This method holds the interfacing securely enough so that it won't slip or shift when you begin fusing.

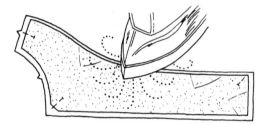

• If you sometimes skip preshrinking your fabric, always be sure to preshrink it when fusible interfacing is to be used. If you don't, and it shrinks the first time you wash your garment after interfacing is applied, it could become distorted in the interfaced areas.

• If you have interfacing left over when you finish your project, roll it on paper towel or wrapping paper tubes to keep it wrinkle-free. Wrap the instructions with it, and label the tube as to interfacing weight so you can find what you need in a hurry for future projects.

FUSIBLE INTERFACING CHART

This chart provides a general sampling of the fusible interfacings that are most readily available in today's market. It is not, however, a complete listing. The interfacings listed have been categorized according to their recommended use for various fabric types and weights. For best results, carefully follow manufacturer's instructions for application and care, and be sure your fabric and interfacing are compatible in fiber content and weight. Always make a test sample before applying fusible interfacing to your garment. Vogue does not assume responsibility for the quality or performance of the interfacings listed below; please contact the manufacturers directly with any questions or concerns (see addresses below).

Use	Interfacing	Fiber Content	Color(s)
Sheer, delicate fabrics, patterns with "soft" details such as gathers, shawl collars, cowl necklines, blouson waists	● 907F Sheer Blenders	100% Polyester	Red, Blue, Silver, Charcoal
	○ So Sheer™	100% Polyester	White, Beige, Charcoal
	□ Jiffy Flex™ Super Lt. Wt.	100% Polyester	White
	△ Sheer Fuse®	100% Polyester	Printblender, White, Beige, Lt. Charcoal
	△ Easy Knit®	100% Nylon	White, Black, Beige, Grey
Sheer, delicate fabrics, patterns with "crisp" details such as shirt collars, plackets	● 906F Sheerweight	100% Polyester	White, Beige
	□ Poly-O™	100% Polyester	White, Beige, Charcoal
Lightweight blouse and dress fabrics, patterns with "soft" details such as gathers, shawl collars, cowl necklines	● 880F Sof-Shape (all bias)	100% Nylon	White
	○ Uni-Stretch Lt. Wt.	75% Polyester 15% Nylon 10% Rayon	White
	□ Woven Fusible	100% Cotton	White, Black
	△ Sure Fuse®	65% Polyester 35% Rayon	White
Lightweight blouse and dress fabrics, patterns with "crisp" details such as shirt collars, band fronts, shirtwaist and coat dresses	● 911FF Featherweight (all bias)	100% Polyester	White, Grey
	● 950F Shirtailor	100% Polyester	White
	○ Fashion Former Lt. Wt.	70% Polyester 30% Rayon	White
	□ Jiffy Flex™ Lt. Wt.	80% Polyester 20% Nylon	White
	□ Fusible Shirt Maker™	100% Spunbonded Polyester	White
	△ Easy Shaper® Lt. Wt.	70% Polyester 20% Nylon 10% Rayon	White, Charcoal
	△ Shirt Fuse®	100% Polyester	White, Beige, Charcoal
	△ Shape-Flex® All Purpose	100% Cotton	White, Black

Use	Interfacing	Fiber Content	Color(s)
Medium weight woven blouse, dress and sportswear fabrics, lightweight suitings	● 70F Shapewell Woven	100% Woven Cotton	White
	● 911FF Featherweight (all bias)	100% Polyester	White, Grey
	● 880F Sof-Shape (all bias)	100% Nylon	White
	● 921 Stretch Ease™	90% Polyester 10% Nylon	White
	● 931TD Tri-Dimensional Med. Wt. to Heavywt.	50% Polyester 50% Nylon	White
	○ Fusible P-91	100% Cotton	White
	○ Detail Fusible	70% Polyester 30% Rayon	White
	○ Armo-Weft	60% Polyester 40% Rayon	White, Black, Beige, Grey
	○ SRF™ (Stretch Recovery Fabric)	75% Polyester 25% Nylon	White, Charcoal
	○ Uni-Stretch Suit Wt.	75% Polyester 15% Nylon 10% Rayon	White
	○ Fashion Former Med. Wt.	70% Polyester 30% Nylon	White
	○ Whisper Weft	60% Polyester 40% Rayon	White, Beige, Dk. Grey
	□ Jiffy Flex™ Lt. Wt.	80% Polyester 20% Nylon	White, Black
	□ Jiffy Flex™ Suit Wt.	80% Polyester 20% Nylon	White, Black
	△ Shape-Flex® All Purpose	100% Cotton	White, Black
	△ Easy Shaper® Suit Wt.	70% Polyester 20% Nylon 10% Rayon	White, Charcoal
	△ Tailor's Touch®	70% Polyester 20% Nylon 10% Rayon	White, Charcoal
Suit and coating fabrics, "soft" details such as shawl collars, wrap closings, blouson styling	● 880F Sof-Shape	100% Nylon	White
	○ Armo-Weft	60% Polyester 40% Rayon	White, Black, Beige, Grey
	○ Whisper Weft	60% Polyester 40% Rayon	White, Beige, Dk. Grey
	□ Woven Fusible	100% Cotton	White, Black
	△ Easy Shaper® Suit Wt.	70% Polyester 20% Nylon 10% Rayon	White, Charcoal
	△ Shape-Flex® All Purpose	100% Cotton	White, Black

Use	Interfacing	Fiber Content	Color(s)
Suit and coating fabrics, "crisp" details, tailored silhouette	● 881F Pel-Aire	100% Nylon	Natural, Grey
	○ Fusible Acro	51% Polyester 43% Rayon 6% Goathair	Natural
	□ Jiffy Flex™ Suit Wt.	80% Polyester 20% Nylon	White, Black
	△ Tailor's Touch®	50% Polyester 50% Rayon	White, Black
	△ Suit Shape®	60% Polyester 40% Nylon	White, Grey
	△ Easy Shaper® Suit Wt.	70% Polyester 20% Nylon 10% Rayon	White, Charcoal
Knits Only (Lightweight)	● 921 Stretch-Ease™	90% Polyester 10% Nylon	White
	● 880F Sof-Shape (all bias)	100% Nylon	White, Grey
	○ Uni-Stretch Lt. Wt.	75% Polyester 15% Nylon 10% Rayon	White
	○ Whisper Weft	60% Polyester 40% Rayon	White, Beige, Dk. Grey
	○ Fashion Former Lt. Wt.	70% Polyester 30% Rayon	White
	□ Jiffy Flex™ Lt. Wt.	80% Polyester 20% Nylon	White, Black
	△ Easy Knit®	100% Nylon	White, Black, Beige, Grey
Knits Only (Medium to Heavyweight)	● 931TD Tri-Dimensional Med. Wt. to Heavy Wt.	50% Polyester 50% Nylon	White
	○ SRF™ (Stretch Recovery Fabric)	75% Polyester 25% Nylon	White, Charcoal
	○ Uni-Stretch Suit Wt.	75% Polyester 15% Nylon 10% Rayon	White
	○ Fashion Former Med. Wt.	70% Polyester 30% Rayon	White
	□ Jiffy Flex™ Suit Wt.	80% Polyester 20% Nylon	White, Black
	△ Easy Knit®	100% Nylon	White, Black, Beige, Grey

● **Pellon Corp.,** 119 W. 40th St., New York, NY 10018 (212) 391-6300
○ **Crown Textile Co./Armo,** 1412 Broadway, New York, NY 10018 (212) 391-5880
□ **Staple Sewing Aids,** 141 Lanza Ave., Garfield, NJ 07026 (800) 631-3820
△ **Stacy Fabrics Corp.,** Educational Dept., 38 Passaic St., Wood-Ridge, NJ 07075 (201) 779-1121

WOVEN FUSIBLES

Woven fusible interfacings have a grainline. The lengthwise direction is the stable direction and should be laid out as your fabric is, according to the grainline arrows on the pattern pieces.

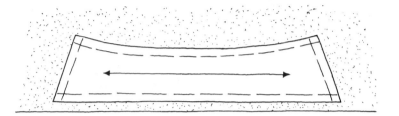

Woven fusible interfacings have stretch, or give, in the crosswise direction. They can be used with woven fabrics and with moderate-stretch knit fabrics in stable areas such as collars. When you need a little more stretch or flexibility at an interfaced section and you're using a woven fusible interfacing, cut it on the crosswise grain instead of the lengthwise grain.

NON-WOVEN FUSIBLES

All-bias fusible interfacings that are non-woven have no grainline and can be cut in any direction. Because of their construction, they won't ravel. Other non-wovens have an in-dicated crosswise and lengthwise grain and may have *extra* stretch in the crosswise grain for use with active wear and stretchier knits.

The general application procedures for non-woven fusibles are the same as for woven fusibles, with specific directions supplied by each manufacturer. They are available in a variety of weights, making it easy to find the right one for your fabric. Since they work equally well with woven and knit fabrics, your choice depends on the overall appearance you want for any particular garment section.

APPLYING FUSIBLE INTERFACING

The general fusing instructions for both woven and non-woven interfacings are the same:

- *Place the coated side of the interfacing on the wrong side of the fabric.*

- *Cover it with a damp press cloth.*

- *With the iron set to the heat recommended in the interfacing instructions, apply plenty of steam and hold the iron in one place for the recommended number of seconds. Never slide the iron. If the garment section is larger than the iron, lift the iron and put it down again next to where it was, slightly overlapping the edge of the first location. Continue across the garment section in this press-and-lift manner until it is fused entirely.*

- *Turn the garment section over and press, in the same manner, for the recommended length of time to remove excess moisture. Let the fabric cool before checking the bond. If you missed a spot, replace the pressing cloth and press for an additional 5 to 10 seconds.*

WAISTBAND INTERFACINGS

Packaged fusible waistband interfacings are easy-to-use time-savers because they are pre-cut. Most have perforations or slots that, when placed on the foldline of your fabric, ensure a sharp, straight fold with no inner construction bulkiness.

Follow these general guidelines for applying them, checking the package directions for specific instructions for your particular brand.

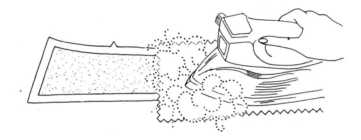

- *Cut the interfacing the length of your waistband pattern piece and trim the ends at the seamline.*

- *Place the interfacing, coated side against the wrong side of your fabric, positioning the perforations along the foldline and the straight edges along the seamlines. Cover it with a damp press cloth and fuse according to the instructions.*

- *To avoid bulk, do not catch the interfacing in the waistline seam when attaching the waistband.*

How to Use Fusible Web

Fusible web has a bonding agent that is similar to that of fusible interfacing in texture but is used to join two layers of fabric rather than to serve as a fabric reinforcement. It is a thin net material and is sold in narrow strips or in wider pieces, by the yard (or meter). There are many ways to use it, for hemming, applying trims and appliqués and fusing facings among them. Fusible web also can be used as a permanent basting for positioning pockets, for example, before stitching.

There are general guidelines for working with fusible web that should be used along with specific product directions.

- *Complete preliminary pressing before positioning the web, making sure hems are measured accurately and are straight and that markings for trims and appliqués are precise and positioned where you want them.*

- *When fusing a hem, place the web 1/4" (6mm) below the edge of the hem allowance. This keeps the soleplate of your iron from touching the web and keeps the hem edge from being outlined on the right side of your garment.*

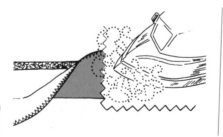 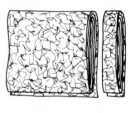

- *Cut long strips of fusible web from a large piece by folding the web several times, measuring the width you need and cutting it with one short snip.*

- *Protect your ironing board cover with an old sheet when working with fusible web to avoid cover cleanups when small pieces stick.*

- *Fusible web can be removed, if necessary, by an application of heat and steam to the bonded area. While the fabric is warm, pull the two layers apart. Continue applying heat and steam until as much of the residue as it is possible to remove is gone. Any that remains may be removed with denatured alcohol—but test your fabric first for alcohol tolerance.*

Use fusible web to mend a rip in a garment invisibly. Align the edges and fuse a pinked piece of self-fabric to the wrong side of the garment, behind the rip.

To give belt carriers extra body and permanent sharp edges, insert a narrow strip of fusible web into the fold of the two layers of fabric.

How to Make Friends with Your Sewing Machine

People who don't love sewing treat their machines like mortal enemies, to be dealt with only when absolutely necessary. Even people who love to sew often don't take the time to understand the intricacies of their machines, using them to perform standard functions and never going beyond the basics. Making friends with your sewing machine is much like making friends with someone you've just met . . . it takes understanding, patience, nurturing, enthusiasm and curiosity. The more you learn, the more you're able to do together. It is impossible to cover here the characteristics of every kind of sewing machine manufactured in the past few decades, but there are some basic tips and guidelines that show how your machine can be a very good friend indeed, making many sewing procedures fast and easy that once were tedious.

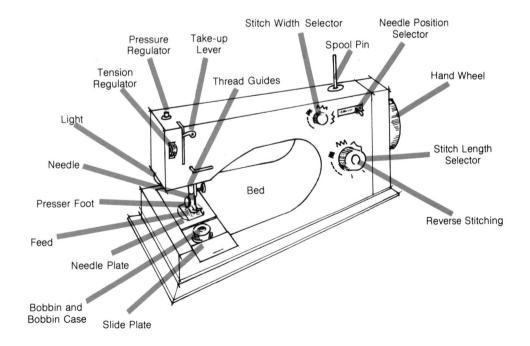

Knowing how to make the necessary adjustments that ensure smooth sewing is a kindness to both you and your machine. You do not have to be a mechanical wizard to keep your sewing machine operating at its optimum capabilities. Begin with the instruction manual or booklet that came with your machine. If you don't have one, write to the manufacturer, listing your machine make and model number, and request a manual. These booklets explain the special qualities and care requirements of your machine, as well as the capabilities of various attachments and the stitching techniques that can be utilized. Most books include a diagram of the machine, which serves as a general reference for the step-by-step directions for using each mechanism.

Easy sewing starts with the essential pieces
that take you from day to night, week to week and
month to month . . . pieces that meet the
fashion demands of your life . . . that are easy
to sew and easy to wear.

Essential tops and bottoms should be able to mix and match with ease. Blend fabric, texture and silhouette and add an easy coat to wear over everything.

Change a good daytime look into one for night by removing the jacket and changing accessories.

A daytime mood changes to an evening one with a change of tops and jewelry. A slim skirt easily does double fashion duty.

Straight, simple jackets cover up a too-bare-for-daytime dress and uncover a perfect look for nighttime. Just change your stockings and accessories for an entirely different mood.

One beautiful blouse goes around the clock. Keep it neutral to make it easy to wear with all your skirts and pants, then dress it up or down.

The careful selection of fabric, each time you sew, gives you clothes that are transitional at least three seasons of the year. Take a traditionally spring fabric, linen, into summer and then add a jacket for fall.

A fall knit three-piece suit becomes a spring blouse and skirt. The same blouse, with lightweight pants or a wool skirt, travels through summer and winter, too.

If you're sewing a lightweight favorite for summer, make a winter weight version at the same time to save cutting and sewing time.

Getaway clothes, whether for a weekend or a week, should give you many fashion looks with a minimum of pieces.

One terrific jacket tops pants and skirts with aplomb— and keeps packing to a minimum, too.

Warm weather getaways should include a sun dress that is equally beautiful in the moonlight . . . just add evening sandals and jewelry.

Keep fabrics easy care and color co-ordinated to multiply mixing and matching possibilities.

There is nothing like the perfect dress for fast dressing and easy confidence. The best dresses are easy to sew and full of easy-to-do designer touches.

There is nothing tricky about any of these pockets and they add a lot of fashion—and convenience—to your dresses.

The right dress goes everywhere you do. Look for simple lines, easy closures and a minimum of seaming and shaping to save extra fitting time.

To save time, instead of sewing waistline seams simply belt in fullness or sew a classic chemise with straight or soft lines.

When your schedule requires going right from the office to an evening out, look for the easy, elegant lines that are appropriate to both.

Fresh makeup and a quick change of accessories are all you need to dress up these business looks for evening.

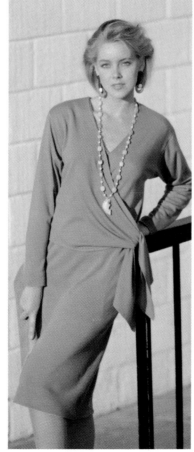

To make one dress do the work of two, use fabrics that wear easily and well and don't wrinkle. Use solid colors or small prints that can move from the office to after-hours occasions with ease.

Classic, timeless suits and fabrics can be made in many shapes and silhouettes. Look for the easy tailoring details of unlined jackets, cardigan fronts or soft lapels and easy fit.

Hem lengths should flatter your proportions. To keep lines straight, take the time to measure carefully. Then the sewing is easy.

Never limit your fashion life by avoiding suits! Every one of these is easy to sew and gives you sophisticated wardrobe additions and great versatility.

Fabulous evenings deserve fabulous fashion. To make it easy, just avoid very slippery or very sheer fabrics that require more sewing time.

Easy designer touches make the best evenings even better. Fluid lines, soft draping and easy, narrow hems all give a couturier look.

Coats and jackets complete your wardrobe. Look for raglan, dolman, full-cut or drop-shoulder sleeves for easy fit and easy sewing.

To make pinning, cutting and sewing easier, use fabrics that give warmth without bulk.

THREAD TENSION

A feature common to all machines, from the oldest to the newest, is a thread tension control. The tension regulates how much thread is fed into every stitch. When the needle pierces the fabric, the thread from the top spool joins and is locked into a loop with the thread from the bobbin. When the thread tension is set just right, the stitches are identical on both sides of the fabric. If the tension is too tight, the thread breaks; if it is too loose, the thread becomes tangled under the feed plate and jams your machine. It actually saves time to test the tension before beginning your project. If you don't check it before you stitch your first dart or seam, you might have to rip out stitches later, which takes much longer.

To test thread tension, stitch about 3" (7.5cm) on a double thickness of a scrap of your fabric. You can check visually by looking at the stitches. If the upper tension is too loose, loops from the top thread form on the bottom of the fabric because too much thread is being fed through the needle into each stitch.

If the upper tension is too tight, loops of bobbin thread form on the top of the fabric because not enough thread is being fed to meet the bobbin or bottom thread. Seams often pucker because of this.

When the tension is adjusted correctly, equal amounts of thread from the spool and bobbin have been drawn so that both threads are balanced on both sides of the fabric and link in the middle of the fabric layers. No loops appear on either side.

Another tension test is to hold your fabric at both ends of the stitching line and tug until one of the threads breaks. Whichever thread breaks is the one that needs tension adjustment. If both threads break, evenly, the tension is balanced and you don't need to make an adjustment.

Never adjust the bobbin tension, unless it is absolutely necessary, because it is pre-set during manufacturing. Check your manual for instructions on repositioning the bobbin tension. Usually an upper tension adjustment corrects the problem. Locate the tension regulator on your machine. On most machines, the higher the number on the dial, the tighter the upper thread tension. The regulator increases or decreases the resistance the thread meets as it moves between the spool and the needle.

If you have a fairly new machine, check your manual to see if one of its features is automatic tension adjustment. If it is, you rarely have to make any adjustments yourself.

FEED AND PRESSURE

The feed mechanism on your machine is the one that interacts with the presser foot to move the fabric under the presser foot, moving it into position for each stitch. The distance the fabric moves is regulated by the stitch length selector. If the stitch length is a basting stitch or the longest stitch your machine makes, the fabric is fed at a faster rate than when the regulator is set for more stitches per inch (2.5cm). Refer to the chart on page 31 for the correct stitch length setting to use with your fabric and thread.

In order for the feed mechanism to work, pressure has to be applied from the presser foot. If you've ever forgotten to lower the presser foot when stitching, you know that the needle goes up and down in one spot. The feed mechanism alone cannot move the fabric.

When the fabric layers move evenly with one another, the feed and pressure are adjusted correctly and the seams are stitched evenly. If there is too much pressure, the top layer of fabric may move faster than the bottom layer, causing uneven seams. If there is too little pressure, the result usually is uneven or skipped stitches or uneven movement of the fabric layers.

The pressure regulator on your machine adjusts the applied force. If your fabric is not feeding evenly through the machine, you may need more pressure. If your fabric is stretching as you sew so that the fabric layers are uneven at the end, you may need less pressure. You shouldn't ever push or pull your fabric under the presser foot. Correctly adjusted feed and pressure do that for you. Your hands should be guiding the fabric only.

TAKING CARE OF YOUR MACHINE

Your sewing machine booklet lists the specific points on your machine that need cleaning and oiling. If you follow these directions and take good care of your machine, it will operate at peak efficiency, require little or no unexpected servicing and last for many, many years. There are three general maintenance procedures that apply to all machines.

- *When you're not using your machine, keep it covered. If you don't want to put it back into its case after each use, cover it with a large plastic bag or a sewing machine cover, available at most sewing machine and notions stores. Or make a cover out of a pretty fabric, similar to a kitchen appliance cover.*

- *Clean your machine each time you have completed a garment to prevent lint buildup.*

- *Keep your machine well oiled so that all the mechanisms move quietly and smoothly, but never over-oil. The wrong kind of oil can damage your machine. Use only the type of oil recommended in the instruction book. If your machine doesn't have its own cleaning tools, you can purchase sewing machine maintenance kits that include such things as a lint brush, an oiler, a sewing machine cover, small screwdrivers and even an extra motor belt in case you need to replace the one on the machine.*

Take the time to check your machine. Make sure the needles are sharp, smooth and clean, and that both needle and bobbin are inserted correctly. Check that the threading is correct and that the stitch length, pressure, feed and tension are adjusted precisely. Together with cleaning and oiling, these few procedures help make sewing faster, easier and trouble-free. It's a small investment compared to the time and money that can be wasted if you don't follow these procedures.

MACHINE EQUIPMENT

Your sewing machine arrives with some basic equipment—usually such things as a zipper foot, a light bulb and bobbins. There are other accessories that are great aids in various sewing projects, such as the special feet mentioned on pages 32–33.

A straight-stitch foot and straight-stitch needle plate generally come with your machine. They give you good fabric control and should be used for straight stitching, edgestitching or when you are sewing with delicate fabrics. The small hole in the needle plate keeps delicate fabrics from being pulled into the machine during stitching.

A general-purpose foot and general-purpose needle plate have a wider hole and opening. They can be used for straight stitching on firm fabrics but must be used for zigzag stitching so the needle has room to swing from side to side.

Needles and thread are sewing machine equipment, too. See pages 28 to 31 for needle and thread descriptions and compatibility, and keep the following tips in mind for each garment you begin:

• *If you notice skipped stitches, it can mean that you are using the wrong type needle, that it is blunt or broken or that it is not properly inserted. It also can mean that the thread is not compatible with your fabric.*

• *If the needle breaks, it can mean that you hit a pin, that the needle is not properly inserted and is coming down at an angle or that the needle is too fine for your fabric.*

• *If you hear a regular thud or thumping noise as you stitch, it usually means that the needle is damaged or broken.*

Look for these causes, and always check that your machine is threaded correctly, both along the machine and in the bobbin, before you become completely frustrated. A sewing machine, like a computer, has to be programmed correctly in order for it to feed the sewing solutions back to you.

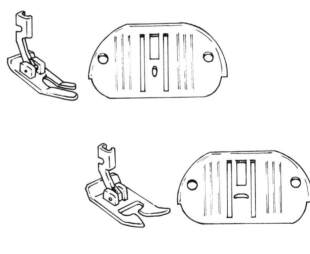

Use a hair dryer to blow lint and fuzz from hard-to-reach places in your sewing machine.

83

MACHINE STITCHES

One of the greatest returns on the investment of a new sewing machine is its ability to perform all sorts of stitches that once were done only by hand. Again, refer to your trusty sewing machine manual for a listing of the stitches your machine produces automatically and those it can produce with the turn of a dial or the addition of an accessory. For example, many machines can zigzag, overcast and blindstitch, and although most easy patterns will not require those techniques, practice them when you have some free time so you can substitute them, if you wish. Practice on scraps, disposable uncoated dust cloths or even paper toweling, remembering to clean away lint afterward, until you become adept at each stitch.

There are several stitches that are used on easy patterns, none of which is difficult and all of which provide construction or decorative finishes. They can be done by all machines and require nothing more than the right thread and needle and a steady hand and eye.

Easestitching

Often a pattern calls for you to ease one layer of fabric as you join it with another, slightly smaller layer. This is done to provide shaping, usually at the shoulder, sleeve or waistline. Easestitching is the procedure that helps you accomplish this. It actually is a gathering stitch but is used to shape specific garment areas rather than large garment sections such as ruffles.

- *Set your machine to a fairly long stitch, about 6 to 8 stitches per inch (per 25mm), and easestitch along the seamline of the larger garment section only. Do not backstitch or tie knots.*

- *Match the markings on the two layers and pin, at the markings or at both ends, being careful not to pin into the stitching.*

- *Pull the bobbin thread, as you would to gather, to ease the fullness until the markings are aligned. Evenly distribute the fullness, and either pin baste or machine baste to hold the easing evenly. Stitch the garment sections together along the seamline.*

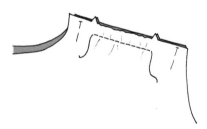

Edgestitching

Edgestitching is a row of stitching applied very close to the finished edge. It is used to keep edges flat along such garment areas as pockets, plackets, pleats, collars and lapels. For example, edgestitching keeps the seam of two fabric layers from rolling to the right side of your garment and keeps pleat edges sharp. Because you are following the natural edge of the garment section, it is easy to maintain an even, straight stitching line. Edgestitching is also used as a decorative stitch.

- *Use the straight-stitch needle plate and foot for control. Since you are stitching right at the edge of the fabric and not in a seam allowance, soft fabrics could be pulled into a general-purpose needle plate. See page 83 for illustrations of both kinds of needle plates.*

Gathering

A softly draped dirndl skirt and a full, billowy one have been gathered at the waistline for fit. Gathering is a very easy procedure, as long as you do it gently and give yourself the timesaving safeguard of two rows of gathering stitches.

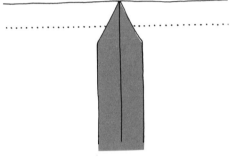

- *Trim crossing seam allowances diagonally, at the gathering lines, to reduce bulk before you gather.*
- *With your fabric right side up, stitch one row at the seamline, leaving long thread ends and being careful to have the stitches just meet but not overlap. Stitch a second row, 1/4" (6mm) above the first, in the seam allowance. Keep the lines parallel and never cross the first row of stitching. This is your safeguard—if the thread breaks on the first row, you can gather the second row without having to stitch again.*

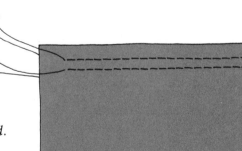

- *Set your machine stitch at its longest length for heavier fabrics and a slightly shorter length for fine fabrics. Loosen the upper thread tension slightly to make it easier to pull the bobbin thread.*

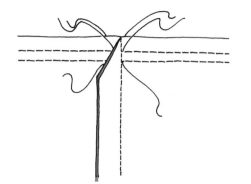

• *If the gathering stitches cross joining seams on large garment sections, such as a skirt, stop the stitches on one side of the seam. Leave long thread ends and resume stitching directly on the other side of the seam.*

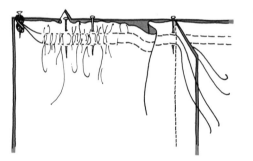

• *When you are stitching a gathered section to one that is not gathered, such as a skirt to its waistband, pin the two sections right sides together, matching the edges and construction markings. With the side to be gathered facing you, pull the bobbin threads from one side, gently sliding the fabric along the threads, adjusting the gathers with your other hand to keep them even.*

• *To keep the bobbin threads from pulling out at the other end, secure them to a pin, winding them in a figure eight. If you are gathering in small sections because you stopped and started again on either side of a cross seam, gather each section and secure the thread ends with pins.*

When gathering, use a different color thread on the bobbin than you're using as a top thread so you immediately can identify which thread to pull.

- *Once the entire section has been gathered and adjusted, pin baste the gathered section to the ungathered section, matching construction markings.*

- *Stitch along the seamline with the gathered side facing you so you can keep the gathers evenly held, to prevent catching tucks or creases in the seam.*

- *If you're gathering around a corner to create a ruffle, keep a little extra fullness at the corner so the ruffle isn't flat-looking.*

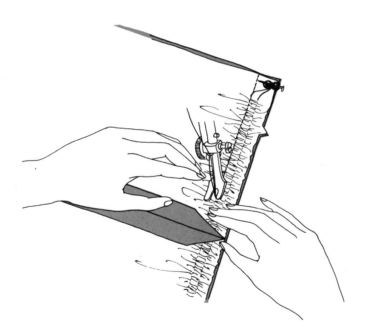

When gathering small areas, don't stop stitching at the end; instead, take two stitches across into the seam allowance and continue the second row of stitches parallel to the seamline 1/4" (6mm) away. This prevents the thread from pulling out.

87

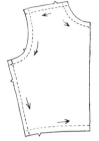

Staystitching

As you handle garment sections that have bias or very curved areas, they can be pulled out of shape, distorted or stretched. To prevent any unwanted stretching, immediately stay-stitch when you remove the pattern tissue from the fabric. Staystitching stabilizes the area so it retains its shape.

- *Use the stitch length and thread you will be using to construct the garment, and stitch about 1/8" (3mm) inside the seamline, in the seam allowance. This distance usually is 1/2" (13mm) from the raw edge.*

- *Don't pull on the fabric as you stitch. Stitch slowly, guiding lightly with your fingers.*

- *Hold the pattern tissue against the area you staystitch to check that they still are identical. If there are any changes, pull the thread to readjust the area.*

To facilitate topstitching around corners and curves, hand baste, using long stitches, along the top-stitching line. This gives you a guide to follow when using the foot or tape is not practical.

Topstitching

Topstitching is one or more lines of stitching along a finished edge. It is an attractive way to emphasize the structural lines of your garment and add fashion detailing easily. Topstitching also keeps edges and seams flat and serves as a construction method for many features, such as pleats, pockets and hems.

- *With the right side of your fabric up, stitch where indicated, using a guide to keep the stitching line straight. Often topstitching is placed 1/4" (6mm) from the edge or seam. Place the outside toe of your presser foot along the edge or seam as a guide for that depth.*

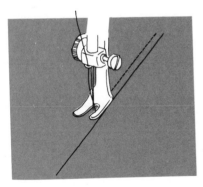

- *If the topstitching is placed more than 1/4" (6mm) from the edge, apply sewing tape along the topstitching line as a guide, being careful not to stitch through the tape.*

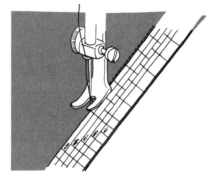

- *A topstitching stitch length, which is about 6 to 8 stitches per inch (per 25mm), usually is longer than the machine stitching you used for constructing the garment. To determine the best length for your project, and to check the thread tension, experiment on a double layer of a scrap of your fabric.*

- *Topstitching can be done after your garment is completed, but the easier way is to do it on each section, during the construction process, while the fabric is still fairly flat. Most easy patterns instruct you to topstitch as you go.*

Understitching

Sometimes a facing or lapel just won't stay flat, the way it is supposed to. If this happens at an area where edgestitching or topstitching would be inappropriate, understitching is an easy way to get the control you need.

- *Grade and clip the seam allowances and press them toward the facing, with the facing opened out.*

- *From the right side of the facing, machine stitch close to the seamline, through all seam allowances. Turn the facing in and press.*

Thread carriers

A belt, tie or sash carrier can be made rapidly and easily by a zigzag sewing machine as a substitute for a fabric carrier.

- *Twist several strands of thread together and cut 1-1/2" (3.8cm) longer than the finished length. Knot both ends.*

- *Hold the twisted threads taut and stitch over them with a zigzag satin stitch, from one end to the other. Pin the carrier in place, between the two layers of fabric, which are pinned right sides together, before you stitch the seam.*

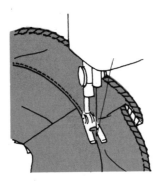
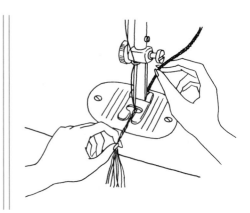

How to Sew by Hand

Even though a tremendous amount of sewing can be done by machine, there are times when it is necessary to sew by hand. There are many intricate hand stitches, used for decorative purposes, in crewel and embroidery, and many machine stitches that can be duplicated by hand stitches, too. Following are the basic stitches used in finishing and sewing fabric. See pages 28 to 31 for pointers on needles and thread, and see page 59 for a review of hand basting.

Backstitch Tack

A backstitch tack is a stronger and more professional way to attach thread to your fabric than is tying a knot, and should be used whenever the thread is permanent. Thread may be knotted for basting stitches, since the thread will be removed and an exposed knot is temporary.

- *Take a small stitch in your fabric at the beginning of any hand sewing and then stitch over the first stitch several times. This secures the thread firmly. Repeat when you come to the end of the thread. Because your thread is not knotted, be careful not to pull it right through the fabric on the first stitch! Hold a short thread end with your fingers when you begin the backstitch tack, to keep it from pulling through. If the thread end is visible when you complete the tack, clip it to be even with the other stitches.*

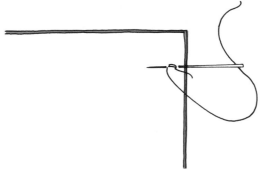

Cut thread on an angle so it will slip more easily through the eye of the needle. Biting or breaking it may seem faster than hunting for scissors, but that makes the thread ends fray so they're hard to get through the needle.

For the most efficient sewing, begin with a single strand of thread that is no longer than 18" to 23" (45cm–60cm), or double that for doubled thread. This length keeps tangles and knots at a minimum and is easier to control than is a longer length.

If your thread becomes twisted, dangle the needle. It automatically turns and untwists the thread. Run your thumb and index finger along the thread to finish the untwisting. Using beeswax strengthens the thread and prevents tangling. Beeswax also makes it easier to thread your needle.

Blindstitch

Because a blindstitch is inconspicuous on the right side of your fabric as well as on the wrong side, it may be used for hemming and holding facings in place.

- *After you finish the raw edges, roll them back about 1/4" (6mm) on the garment as you sew, taking a short, horizontal stitch through one thread on the garment side and then picking up a thread from the hem or facing diagonally above the first stitch. Repeat this diagonal stitching, back and forth. Do not pull the stitches tight.*

Slipstitch

A slipstitch provides an almost invisible finish for hemming and holding pockets and trims in place.

- *Insert the needle through the folded edge and through a thread of the under fabric at the same point. Keep stitches evenly spaced 1/8" to 1/4" (3mm–6mm) apart.*

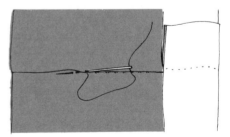

Thread Chain

If you don't have a zigzag stitch on your machine, you can make a thread chain by hand. Thread chains are used for belt carriers or for thread eyes to use with hooks.

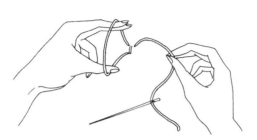

- *Backstitch tack to begin, at the point where the thread chain begins. Take another small stitch and form a loop.*

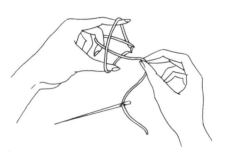

- *Hold the loop open with the thumb and index finger of one hand. With the middle finger of the same hand, reach through the loop and pull the long end of the thread through to form a new loop.*

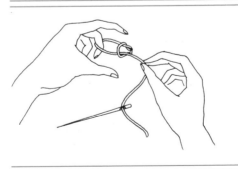

- *Holding the new loop, let the first loop slide off your fingers.*

- *Gently pull both the new loop and the thread until the first loop forms a knot at the base. Continue forming new loops and sliding the loop before it down the thread, keeping the loops even, until you have formed a chain the length you need. Bind off the chain by inserting the needle through the last loop, through the fabric. Backstitch tack to secure the chain end to the fabric.*

Easy Sewing Techniques

If you took a survey among all your friends who sew, each would have at least one construction detail she or he avoids at all cost. One never has pockets in her clothes; another only sews things she can pull on, with nary a buttonhole or zipper in sight; and yet another would tie a rope around her waist before she'd dream of making a belt and carriers to slip it through. As common as it is to have certain sewing phobias, it's totally unnecessary; once you understand how and why a technique works and gather the tools to help you do the job, you can sew anything!

Some construction details, such as hand smocking or bound buttonholes, do take a lot of time, so that even if you know how they work, you may not be able to spare the hours required to complete them. Others only look complicated but actually are neither difficult nor time consuming. They add a lot of fashion, value and function to your garment and, best of all, have easy, shortcut methods that will make you wonder why you never tried them before! Following are the easy how-to's for everybody's foremost sewing phobias, in alphabetical order for fast reference.

Bands

A neckline band is a professional, designer detail that also serves as a functional opening for getting into your garment. There are two easy-to-make neckline bands that are found in easier patterns that also can be substituted for more complicated bands.

ONE-PIECE PLACKET BAND

1. *It is very important to transfer all the markings on the placket pattern piece to your fabric. What takes you a few extra minutes in marking time saves you countless minutes later in sewing time, since each line is a foldline or stitching line you need to follow exactly. Once they're marked, you won't need to stop and measure as you sew.*

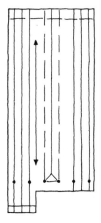

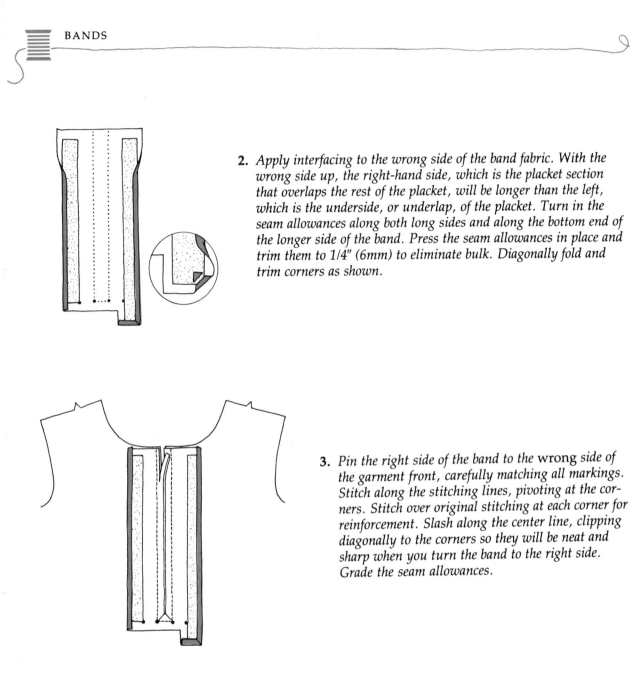

2. *Apply interfacing to the wrong side of the band fabric. With the wrong side up, the right-hand side, which is the placket section that overlaps the rest of the placket, will be longer than the left, which is the underside, or underlap, of the placket. Turn in the seam allowances along both long sides and along the bottom end of the longer side of the band. Press the seam allowances in place and trim them to 1/4" (6mm) to eliminate bulk. Diagonally fold and trim corners as shown.*

3. *Pin the right side of the band to the wrong side of the garment front, carefully matching all markings. Stitch along the stitching lines, pivoting at the corners. Stitch over original stitching at each corner for reinforcement. Slash along the center line, clipping diagonally to the corners so they will be neat and sharp when you turn the band to the right side. Grade the seam allowances.*

4. *Pull the placket through to the right side of the garment. Fold along the foldlines and press. Edgestitch
both long edges of the shorter side, or placket underlap,
to the end of the diagonal clip, making sure you don't
catch the longer side, which overlaps, as you sew.*

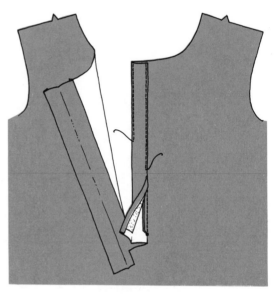

5. *Edgestitch the longer side, or
placket overlap, along both
long edges, ending at the diagonal clip. Keep the underlap
free as you stitch.*

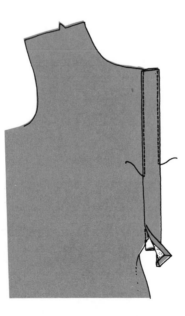

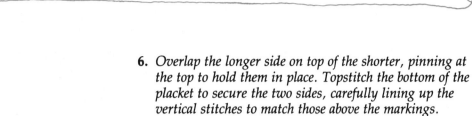

6. *Overlap the longer side on top of the shorter, pinning at the top to hold them in place. Topstitch the bottom of the placket to secure the two sides, carefully lining up the vertical stitches to match those above the markings. Edgestitch around the bottom of the placket.*

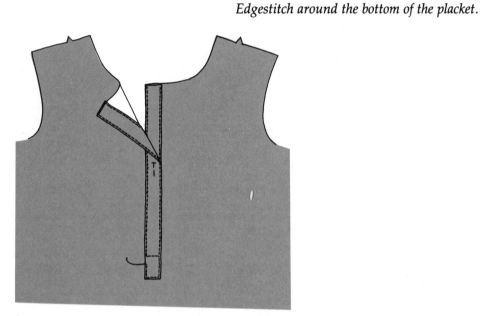

MOCK BAND

To create the appearance of a band on a faced neckline, such as a slit neckline or any finished edge, mark 1–1-1/4" (2.5–3.2cm) from the edge. Then topstitch along the marking.

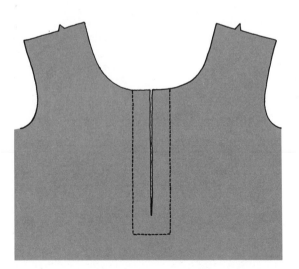

Belts

There are many kinds of belts to sew, out of all kinds of fabrics. The easiest to make is a fold-and-stitch tie belt made out of the same fabric you use for your dress, jacket, skirt or pants or made from a coordinating or contrasting fabric.

Patterns that feature tie belts include the pattern piece. If you don't have a pattern, however, it is easy to figure the length and width of fabric you need. Measured on the straight grain, the belt should be the length of the circumference of your waist plus enough to tie in a bow or knot, with the ends left over plus 1-1/4" (3.2cm) for the end seam allowance. Tie a piece of string or ribbon at your waist the way you plan to tie the belt as a measuring guideline.

The following method is fast and easy because it eliminates the process of turning the belt, since it is done from the right side. The width is double the finished width you want, plus 1-1/4" (3.2cm) for the seam allowances on both long edges.

1. *Press 5/8" (15mm) to the wrong side on all four edges, pressing the long sides first and then pressing the short ends over the sides.*

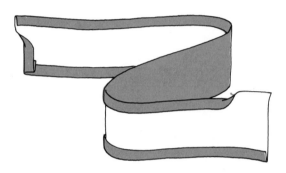

2. *If your fabric is bulky, trim away excess fabric at the corners and miter them. Open out the fabric at each corner and refold it diagonally, keeping the pressed edges flat (A). Diagonally trim away most of the corner to the raw edges of the seam allowance and refold the sides and ends, as they were. The edges now will meet but not overlap (B).*

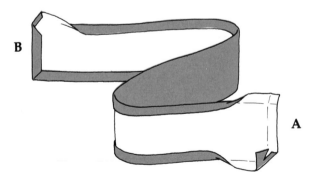

3. Fold the belt in half lengthwise with the **wrong** sides together, matching the edges. Pin baste where the edges meet and press the crease at the fold.

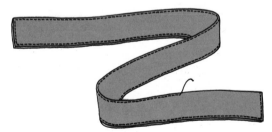

4. Edgestitch through all the layers around all sides of the belt, holding it gently both in front of and behind the presser foot to keep it from twisting as you sew.

Belt Carriers

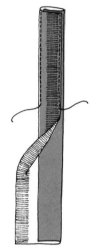

To keep your belt in place when you're wearing it, add belt carriers to your garment. They are attached, by this easy method, after your garment is constructed.

To determine the length for each loop, measure the width of the belt, double it and add 1/4" to 1/2" (6mm–13mm), depending on the thickness of the belt fabric and the carrier fabric. If the fabrics are thick, make the carrier a little longer so the belt can slip through easily without pulling. The width you need is three times the finished width you want.

Cut one long straight strip the total length needed for all loops, and seam allowances if required, on the selvage edge of your fabric for an automatically finished edge.

1. *To fold the fabric in thirds, first fold the raw edge and then the selvage edge so you have two folds with the selvage edge on top. Press the folded fabric and edgestitch both long edges in place. Cut into individual lengths.*

2. *Bring the ends of each loop together and hand sew them. Position the finished carrier with the joined ends centered against your garment. Sew the carrier to your garment at both ends of the loop.*

To make sure carriers are placed evenly around your garment, measure and mark equal distances on each side of a waistline seam or at the top and bottom of a waistband. Check that carrier placement is at intervals that support the belt evenly without allowing it to droop.

Another kind of belt carrier is a thread carrier. See page 90 for the easy machine zigzag method and page 93 for a handmade thread chain.

Binding

Any raw edge can be finished fast with the application of double-fold bias tape or foldover braid. Available in packages and sometimes by the yard, in a variety of colors and widths, these bindings have finished edges and are folded off center. They are folded this way so that the side to be applied to the wrong side of your garment is slightly wider than the side for the right side of your garment. This ensures that both sides are stitched securely when you edgestitch from the right side. Prepare your garment by trimming away the seam allowance close to the stitching line where the binding is to be applied. Because it is impossible to package one continuous bias strip economically, most bindings have seamlines where strips have been stitched together, end to end. Try to plan these seams at inconspicuous areas, when you can.

1. *Always pre-shape the binding to follow the contours of your garment, before you apply it. Steam press it to shrink out any excess fullness that might cause tucks or puckers.*

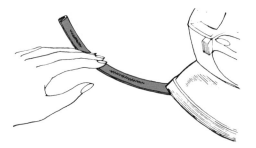

2. *To bind straight and curved edges, encase the trimmed garment edge with the folded bias strip or braid, placing the wider side of the strip on the wrong side of the garment and centering the fold on the cut edge. Edgestitch from the right side through all layers, opening the fold and turning under the ends so they meet when you need to finish the raw edges of the binding. Always leave about 2" (5cm) extra binding free at each end to allow for finishing, trimming what you don't need before turning the ends under.*

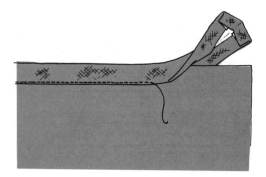

3. *To bind outward squared corners without a pucker, first position braid or binding on one garment edge, as for curved and straight edges, and edgestitch through all layers.*

   Next, turn the binding around the corner, as illustrated, and pin it in place.

   Then miter the corner by folding the excess binding up, forming a diagonal line, and pin the corner. Edgestitch through all layers along the lower edge and then along the mitered fold, or finish the miter by slipstitching.

Buttons

Buttons are fasteners that also add decorative touches to your garments. There are stores that specialize in buttons—hand-painted porcelain buttons; gold buttons; brass buttons; square, round, flower-petal and triangular-shaped buttons; and buttons of all sizes, from tiny pearl "baby" buttons to very large coat buttons. Sewing on a button is something even non-sewers can do, but there are easy methods that some professional sewers don't use because they haven't learned the techniques. Certain buttons may be applied by zigzag machine, while others must be sewn on by hand.

BY MACHINE

You may have had a sewing machine with a zigzag stitch and button foot for years and never known you could apply sew-through buttons by machine quickly and easily.

1. *Position the button on its marking and secure it with transparent tape or use a glue stick. Set the needle position to the left and set the zigzag width to align with the holes on the button. Use a special needle plate to cover the feed dogs, lower them, or change the stitch length to 0 to prevent the fabric from moving forward. A shank allows a smooth closure and keeps the fabric from pulling unevenly around the buttons. If you want to make a shank, put a toothpick or a thick machine needle on top of the button, between the holes, and through the special groove in the front of the foot.*

Sew the button, operating your machine slowly so you can check that the button is held in position and so you can control the movement of the needle.

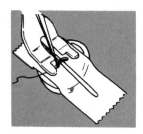

Children who are learning to dress themselves are hard on buttons . . . sew buttons on their clothes with elastic thread to allow a little extra give for little fingers.

Sew an extra button to an inside seam. If you lose one from your garment, you'll have an easy-to-find matching replacement.

For a visual aid when you're button shopping, make a sample buttonhole on a fabric scrap from your garment. Try different buttons through the buttonhole until you find the one that looks just right.

2. Remove the needle or tooth-pick, lift the button away from the fabric and wind the thread firmly around the stitches to form the shank.

BY HAND

Sew-through buttons may be sewn by hand, too. This can be a portable project and done while you are watching television, waiting for an appointment or talking on the telephone, so you can get double duty out of one block of time.

1. Use a double strand of thread for strength and speed. If the thread tends to twist or knot, pull it through beeswax before starting.

2. First, backstitch tack right on the marking for button placement.

3. Insert the needle through one of the holes of the button, going back and forth between the holes until it's secured.

4. If you want a thread shank, sew over a toothpick on top of the button, as you did for machine-sewn buttons, following the procedure for twisting the

thread after sewing is complete.

Shank buttons must be sewn on by hand, but, as their name indicates, they already have a loop or shank on the back, usually of plastic or metal, which provides the space between the button and the fabric that prevents pulled or puckered fabric.

1. Align the direction of the shank with the direction of your buttonhole marking, either vertically or horizontally. Using a double strand of thread, backstitch tack on the button marking on the right side of the fabric.

2. Sew through the shank and then the fabric, repeatedly and evenly, to attach the button. Backstitch into the fabric to secure the thread firmly, and clip the thread close to the garment.

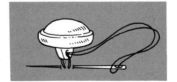

Cut hand button-sewing time in half by using a full strand of embroidery floss with a large-eye needle. Just stitch through each hole twice and secure the floss by tying a knot.

If you use doubled thread to sew on buttons, knot each thread end separately to prevent knotting and twisting.

When your or your children's garments get rough and tough wear, sew on buttons with dental floss. It's also a quick method—twice around, using a big needle, and the button is on for good!

109

Buttonholes

The thought of sewing a buttonhole is one that often strikes terror into the hearts of sewers, either because they never have tried to make one and it seems intimidating, or because they tried one once and it didn't turn out the way they wanted it. Machine buttonholes are not at all difficult, but it is a good idea to practice two or three so you understand how to control the width of your stitches.

For women's garments that close in the front, the buttonholes are on the right side; for those that close in the back, the buttonholes are on the left-hand side. Buttonholes for men's garments are on the left front.

1. *Buttonholes are positioned first in three key places—the neck, the fullest part of the bust and the waist. The remaining buttonholes are spaced evenly between these points. If you have to lengthen or shorten the garment area where the buttonholes are placed, you may have to respace the buttonholes. Do this by measuring new markings before you begin constructing the garment, after the alteration is complete.*

Use interfacing to back buttonholes that is compatible in color and weight to your garment fabric. When your fabric is dark, use a dark interfacing. White interfacing used with dark fabric might show when you cut the buttonhole open.

Use the buttonhole guide that is included in some patterns or a buttonhole spacer, available at notion stores, for fast measuring and spacing of buttonholes, either to mark your fabric according to the pattern or to respace if you have made pattern alterations.

2. Buttonholes are marked according to the buttonhole placement line on the pattern, so that when the two halves of your garment meet, they'll meet and match at the center line when the garment is buttoned. Horizontal buttonholes, which extend 1/8" (3mm) beyond the placement line, are marked with a horizontal line. They have the most give and gap the least when the garment is worn. Vertical buttonholes, used most often on narrow plackets, are placed directly on the buttonhole placement line.

3. Because you stitch buttonholes with the right side of the fabric facing up, markings have to be on the right side. Tailor's chalk or a marking pencil can be used (test them on a scrap of your fabric first), or you can use transparent tape. Cut two pieces and place them about 1/4" (6mm) apart. Mark the exact buttonhole length on the tape. Tape also serves as an excellent guide if your sewing machine does not stitch buttonholes automatically, because it gives you perfectly parallel lines a correct distance from one another.

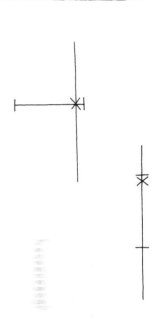

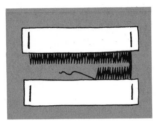

4. Buttonhole attachments and/or zigzag methods vary from machine to machine. Practice making a few buttonholes, following the instructions in your sewing machine manual. Layer your sample exactly the way you will your garment—fabric, interfacing, fabric—using the same fabric and interfacing as used in your garment. After the buttonhole is stitched, cut through all layers of the center of it with small, very sharp scissors or buttonhole scissors. Because it's easy to slip, put a pin at each end of the buttonhole—they will stop your scissors from cutting too far.

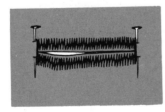

When sewing knits, use vertical buttonholes whenever you can. The lengthwise grain is less stretchy, so the bulk of the buttonhole stitching goes with the rib and is less likely to pucker.

Purchase the same size buttons as recommended on your pattern envelope to save time and avoid remeasuring. The markings on the pattern tissue are already measured and positioned for this size and need only to be traced or transferred.

For a smoother and flatter buttonhole, stitch around the buttonhole twice. Use a narrow stitch width the first time and a wider width the second time.

111

Casings

A casing is an easy fashion detail that helps control fullness in a garment, usually at the neckline, waistline or sleeve edge. There are two basic types of casings, applied and folded, both of which are closed tunnels of fabric that encase a drawstring or an elastic. Refer to pages 132–133 for how to reinforce openings for drawstrings.

APPLIED

An applied casing is made by sewing a separate strip of fabric or single-fold bias tape to your garment. The casing material should be slightly wider than your elastic or drawstring. If you are using a fabric strip, cut it the width of the elastic plus 3/4" (20mm). Fold each long edge 1/4" (6mm) to the wrong side and press. Purchased bias tape is pre-folded for you.

An applied casing, when attached at the waistline or away from the edge of the garment, often is called an off-the-edge casing. If it is attached at the edge of a garment section, such as a sleeve or pant leg, often it is referred to as an on-the-edge casing.

Off the Edge

1. *Pin the bias tape or fabric strip to the garment section along the placement markings indicated on your pattern tissue. Turn under the short ends so they meet but don't overlap. These ends are the openings through which the elastic is drawn. Edgestitch both long edges of the casing, insert and attach the elastic, then slipstitch the opening closed.*

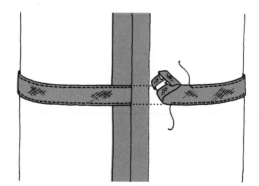

On the Edge

1. To prepare the fabric strip, open out one long edge of your fabric or bias tape without eliminating the foldline or crease line, which you need to see when stitching. Starting at the garment seam, and with right sides together, pin the casing to the garment, with the crease line of the casing along the seamline of the garment. Turn under the ends so the folds meet without overlapping.

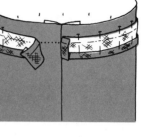

2. Stitch along the crease of the casing. Trim the seam allowance even with the edge of the casing.

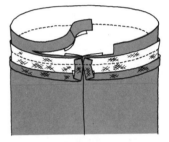

3. Turn the casing to the wrong side of the garment, making sure it does not extend below the garment edge. Press and then edgestitch the folded edge of the casing to the garment. After the elastic is inserted through the opening, pulled through and secured, the casing ends should be slipstitched closed.

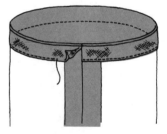

FOLDED

A folded casing is an extension of the garment that is turned to the inside and stitched in place.

Machine baste (A) or fuse the seam allowances to your gar- ment along the casing area (B), so they don't block or catch the elastic when you pull it through the finished casing.

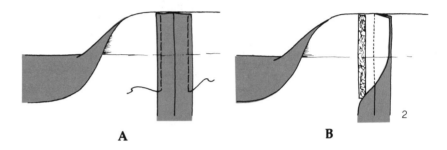

A   **B**

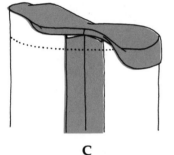

C

1. *Turn the raw edge under 1/4" (6mm), press and then fold the fabric to the wrong side along the foldline, and press again (C).*

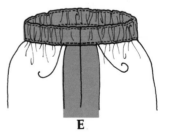

D

2. *Beginning and ending either side of a seamline, edgestitch the turned-under edge to form the casing. Edgestitching the other side of the casing all the way around helps prevent the elastic from twisting or rolling during wearing (D).*

After the elastic has been inserted, pulled through and secured, the casing opening should be edgestitched closed. Carefully line up the stitches with the stitching you've already done and sew closed (E).

E

ELASTIC

If your pattern requires elastic, the instruction sheet tells you how to measure the proper length for your size. As a general rule, measure the body area where it will be worn, such as your wrist, waist or ankle, and add 1/2" (13mm).

1. *To insert elastic through the opening in the casing, attach a bodkin or safety pin to one end and insert it into the casing. Pin the other end to the seam at the opening, with a straight pin, to keep it from being pulled through the casing. Push the bodkin or safety pin through the casing; as it moves it pulls the elastic along with it. Work slowly so that the elastic stays flat and doesn't twist.*

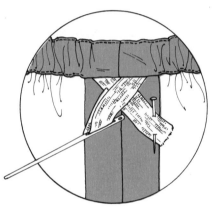

2. *When the elastic is threaded through the casing and the ends meet, unpin both and overlap them 1/2" (13mm). Pin them together evenly, and stitch several times across. Adjust the elastic, again without twisting, to pull the stitched ends inside the casing. Edge-stitch the casing opening closed.*

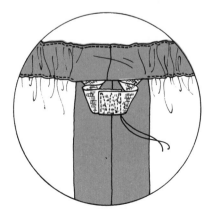

For double-quick elastic insertion, leave two openings in your casing, one at each side seam. Attach a safety pin at each elastic end and insert both of them at one opening. Pull one to the right and one to the left until they meet at the second opening. Secure the elastic and finish the casing at both openings.

115

Collars

In most cases, the first part of you that someone looks at is your face—your eyes, in particular—and everything that is in proximity to your face, including your collar. Both your collar and your hair frame your face. Although hairstyles are not the issue here, you should consider not only the way you wear your hair, but the length and shape of your neck, too, when planning the styles of collars that are the most flattering. And you should pay strict attention to the way you sew and finish the collars you make, since they are such an important part of the first impression you make.

It is easy to do a good job making a collar. Symmetry, smooth and even edges and sharp points are not at all difficult to achieve when you understand the construction techniques for each style.

All collars have two things in common—a top and a bottom, usually called the upper collar and the under collar. Often the under collar is referred to as the collar facing.

The inside shape or inner curve of the collar as it relates to the neckline curve of the bodice is what determines the collar type. The more similar the curves are, the flatter the collar is. A Peter Pan collar is an example of a flat collar. Flat collars are used most commonly on dresses, blouses and in children's wear.

The less alike the neckline curve and the collar curve are, the more the collar stands up. A man's shirt collar with a stand and a mandarin collar are two examples of a standing collar.

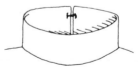

An easy guide for stitching perfect collar curves and corners is to trace the seamline lightly on the interfacing before applying it.

When the two curves differ slightly, the collar stands up slightly and then falls. This is called a rolled collar. Shawl collars and notched collars are two examples of rolled collars.

Most collars are interfaced for shape support. Make sure the weight of the interfacing is compatible with the weight of your fabric. Refer to the chart on pages 73–75 for interfacing selection. When interfacing a pointed collar, trim 1/2" (13mm) off all outer edges of the interfacing and cut the interfacing corners on the diagonal before fusing, to eliminate bulk and to ensure sharp points. Fuse the interfacing to the wrong side of the undercollar. To brush up on fusible interfacing techniques, see page 77.

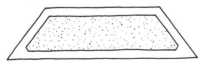

CORNERS AND CURVES

No matter what kind of collar you sew, it has either corners or curves, both of which are easy to achieve perfectly.

1. *Always stitch both sides in the same direction. The direction in which you stitch often determines the way a garment section falls, curves or curls. Stitch from the center back to the front on one half of the collar and then from the center back to the front on the second half.*

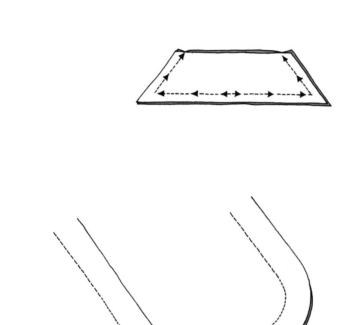

2. *When you reach the corners or curves, reinforce them, using shorter stitches, approximately 15 to 20 per inch (per 25mm), for about 1" (25mm) on either side of the point or curve. This helps prevent any fabric threads from pulling out and fraying when the collar is turned right side out, and allows you to trim close to the stitching to eliminate bulk.*

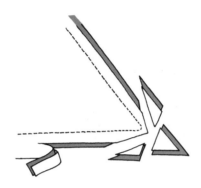

3. *To reinforce corners so threads don't poke out when the corner is turned right side out and so you can trim as close as possible to the corner, take one or two smaller stitches diagonally across the point. Because this stitching is on the inside, it does not interfere with the point when you turn the collar.*

4. *To make turning points easier place a knotted thread between the collar layers with the tail end of the thread facing toward the collar. Stitch over the thread at the point as you sew the collar pieces together. Use this thread tail to pull the corner points out. Remove the thread after turning.*

5. *So that outside curves are smooth and even and so there is more room for the curve to follow its natural shape when it is turned right side out, grade and then notch the seam allowance after stitching.*

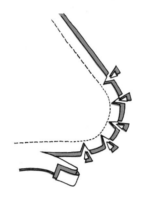

6. *The last thing you want to see peeking out around the edges of your collar is the under-collar. To keep it where it belongs, understitch the seam allowances from the center back to as close to each collar point as is possible. To do this, machine stitch close to the seamline, through all seam allowances from the right*

side. After understitching, press the collar, favoring the upper collar by rolling the seam slightly to the under-collar side. When you do this, the undercollar, because it has been pushed forward, will extend a small distance beyond the upper collar, at the neckline or raw edge. Trim it even with the upper collar edge, baste the two edges together and stitch according to your pattern instructions.

Two easy techniques for applying collar sections to your garment are the sandwiched construction method, when there is a facing, and the edge-stitched construction method, when there is no facing, which includes shortcut steps for finishing.

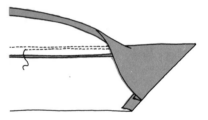

SANDWICH COLLAR CONSTRUCTION

To prevent it from stretching out of shape, your pattern instructions will instruct you to staystitch the neckline edge on your garment section. See page 88 for information.

1. *With the undercollar against the right side of the garment, pin and then machine baste the collar to the neckline, matching notches and other construction marks. If the upper collar appears to have excess fullness or "bubbles" in this position, clip the garment neckline.*

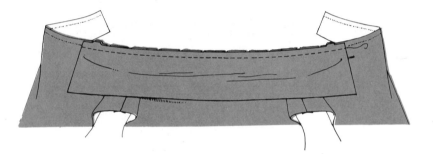

2. *Stitch the front and back facing sections together, then finish the unnotched edge. Place the facing over the collar, right sides together. Position it so that all the neckline edges are even and all construction marks match. Clip the facing seam allowance at the neckline edge, if necessary. Securely pin baste or machine baste the facing in place.*

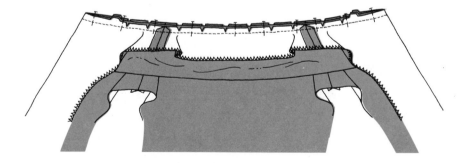

3. *Stitch the collar to the garment.*

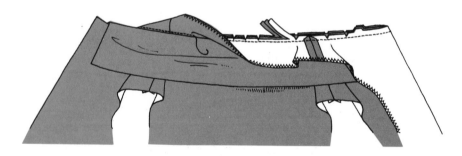

4. *Grade the neckline seam allowance, clipping to the seamline through all layers. Turn the facing to the inside and press. Understitch the facing to the seam allowance, close to the neckline seam, and to within 1" (25mm) of each end.*

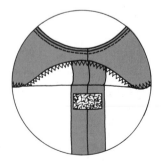

Although the understitching helps keep the facing from rolling out or sticking up, sew it at each shoulder seam. A small piece of fusible web also is a good anchor. See page 78 for application instructions.

EDGESTITCHED COLLAR CONSTRUCTION

Many collars may be edgestitched to the garment. If your garment has other visible top-stitching or edgestitching, this is an excellent choice of collar construction.

1. *Staystitch the garment neckline. Interface (see page 70) one collar section. Trim the neckline seam allowance of one collar section to 1/4" (6mm). Press to the wrong side along the seamline. Stitch both collar sections, right sides together, leaving the neck edge open. Trim and turn the collar right side out and press.*

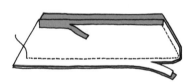

2. *Place the right side of the untrimmed collar section to the right side of the garment neckline, matching notches and other construction markings. Pin baste or machine baste the collar in place, clipping the garment neckline if necessary. Stitch only from one collar seamline to the other, being careful not to catch the trimmed collar section in the stitching.*

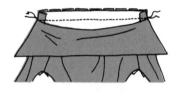

3. *Grade and clip the seam allowance. Fold the free edge of the trimmed collar over the seam allowance and position it at the seamline, positioning the seam allowance between the two collar layers. Pin the collar in place and edgestitch along the neckline edge, with the upper collar up.*

Corners

The practice of "cutting corners" is exactly what these procedures for perfect, sharp, mitered corners are all about. They are used for pointed collars and other seamed areas with corners and are used in tandem with narrow, stitched hems to give a fine, professional finish to your garment.

IN ENCLOSED SEAMS

Although collars are shown in the illustrations, this method also applies to any enclosed seam, such as a facing, cuff or band.

1. *To prepare the corner on an enclosed seam, increase the number of stitches per inch (per 25mm) to 15 to 20 on either side of the corner. This strengthens the area to allow you to trim close to the stitching. Remember to pivot across the corner point, taking one or two stitches diagonally, to reinforce it.*

2. *Trim and grade the seam allowances and trim off the corner point seam allowance close to the stitching.*

3. *First press the seam flat the way it was stitched and then open, using a point presser to facilitate pressing at the corner.*

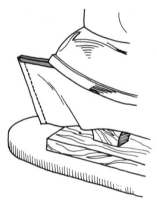

4. *Fold the seam allowances under and press. The corner, instead of having overlapped edges, which can be bulky, is mitered when clipped. The seam allowance edges will meet at an angle at the corner.*

AT HEMS

To keep right angle corners at narrow hems from being bulky, the same kind of mitering procedure described for corners in enclosed seams is used, except the finished corner becomes part of the hem and is not encased in a seam.

1. *Turn up and press the hem allowance the amount stated in the instruction sheet or on the pattern tissue. Open it out and fold the corner diagonally to the wrong side and press along the foldline to form a crease.*

2. *Cut off only the tip of the corner, leaving 1/4" to 3/8" (6mm to 10mm) of fabric from the fold.*

3. *Turn under the raw edge so that the edge lies along the crease and press. The side edges will meet at the corner, covering the cut corner, without any bulk. Finish the hem according to pattern instructions or by machine stitching from the wrong side, with the hem facing up.*

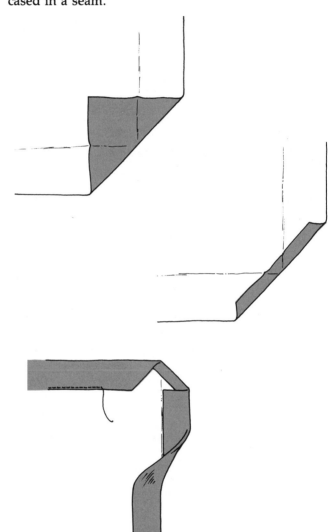

Cuffs

Off the cuff, it is reasonable to say that there are innumerable kinds of cuffs to sew. And there are many ways to attach them, too. Two of the easiest cuffs to make are two of the most classic: extended barrel cuffs, in which the cuff and facing are cut as one piece, and turnback cuffs, made with a deep hem that is folded to the right side of the garment.

To keep both kinds of cuffs well shaped and to give them body, the outer layer, the one with the notch, should be interfaced. Cut a piece of fusible interfacing to extend only to the foldline. Apply interfacing to the notched edge. Fuse in place. Depending on the width of the cuff, pre-cut fusible interfacing can be used. If it is suitable for the cuffs you are sewing, place the perforated lines at the cuff foldlines.

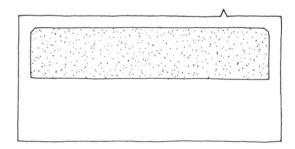

DED BARREL

under 5/8" (15mm) on the side that is not interfaced and Trim to 3/8" (10mm). Place the cuff over the sleeve with the side of the cuff facing the right side of the sleeve, matching ns and notches, with the edge of the interfaced half aligned with e edge of the sleeve. Stitch along the seamline and grade the seam llowance.

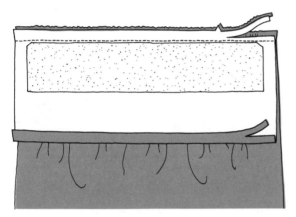

2. Press the seam allowances toward the cuff. Stitch the sleeve seam through the cuff and press open. Turn the cuff to the inside along the foldline, so the wrong sides are together and the folded edge meets the seam covering the seam allowance. Baste close to the upper folded edge to hold it in place. Slipstitch or edgestitch the cuff.

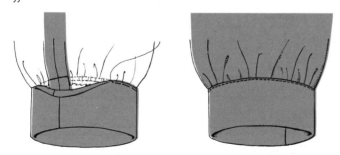

TURNBACK CUFFS

These cuffs, which are used both at sleeve and pant-leg
made with a deep hem that is then folded to the right s
garment. The hem flares slightly so it is larger than the
pant leg at the finished edge. This keeps the sleeve or par
puckering when the cuff is turned back.

1. *To eliminate bulk, trim the seam allowance from the raw*
   the foldline. Finish the raw edge using the method approp
   your fabric.

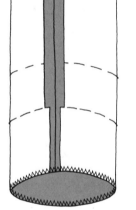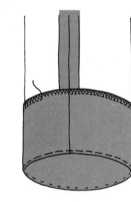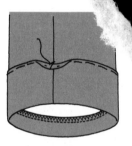

2. *Fold the cuff to the inside along the foldline. Baste close to the*
   foldline. Hem the finished edge. This hem does not show on the
   right side of your garment because the cuff covers the stitching.

3. *Fold the lower edge of the cuff to the right side along the hemline,*
   and tack it in place invisibly so stitches are concealed between both
   layers at each seam.

Darts

Darts are added to your garment construction to help direct and control fullness and to give your garment contours where shaping is needed. The bust, waist and hip all are places where darts are used so your garment follows the curves of your body.

Because darts are measured to fall precisely where they are needed, it is important to transfer markings from your pattern tissue accurately. See page 24 for types of marking tools and page 56 for tips on how to use them.

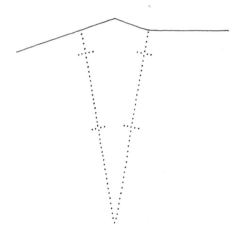

If you are not using a tracing wheel to draw a straight, perfectly tapered dart, hold a 3" × 5" (7.5cm × 12.5cm) card or straight paper edge between the dart markings. Stitch along the straight edge of paper.

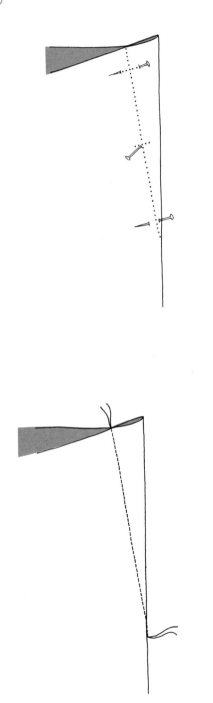

1. *Fold your fabric at the dart, right sides together. To make sure the markings are matched, insert a pin straight through the mark on one side. If it exits through the mark on the other side, they match. If it doesn't, adjust the fold until it does. Pin across the stitching line to hold the dart in place for stitching.*

2. *Stitch darts from the wide end, tapering to nothing at the pointed end with the last two or three stitches on the fold. If you don't taper this way and stitch from the second dart marking abruptly to the point instead, your finished dart point is concave instead of convex and puckers or bubbles.*

   Never backstitch at a dart point. Instead, tie a knot to secure the thread, working the knot to lie flat at the end of the dart.

3. *Press the edge of the dart flat, as it was stitched, and then, because it is a curved detail, press it over a curved surface, such as a pressing mitt or tailor's ham.*

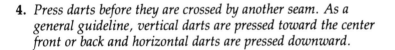

4. *Press darts before they are crossed by another seam. As a general guideline, vertical darts are pressed toward the center front or back and horizontal darts are pressed downward.*

To tie a perfect knot at a dart point or anywhere else, place a pin at the point of the knot and slide the thread down the pin. The thread tightens exactly at the point of the pin and lies flat against the fabric.

Drawstrings

Cords, self-fabric tubes, ribbons and a great variety of other materials, like leather strips, can be used as drawstrings. They serve to gather in the fullness of your garment, usually at the waist or neck, and are pulled through a casing and tied. Drawstrings should be equal in length to the measurement of your body at the point of the casing plus enough extra length for knotting or tying a bow.

To make a self-fabric drawstring, first determine how wide the opening for the drawstring will be.

If you use the selvage of the fabric for one long edge of the drawstring you will have one automatically finished edge. Using this method, cut your fabric three times the width of the opening, and the required length.

1. *Turn each short end 1/4" (6mm) to the wrong side and press.*

2. *Fold the long edges in thirds, turning the raw edge first, then folding the selvage edge so it's on top. Press the folded edges, then edgestitch all edges.*

If you don't use the selvage, simply cut a strip of fabric two times the width of the opening, plus 1/2" (13mm) for turning under the raw edges, and the required length.

1. *Turn each short end 1/4" (6mm) to the wrong side and press.*

2. *Turn each long end 1/4" (6mm) to the wrong side and press. Fold in half lengthwise and press the fold. Edgestitch all edges.*

The casing needs an opening through which the drawstring is first inserted and through which the ends then extend. There are two kinds of openings, which usually can be substituted for one another.

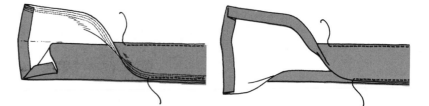

BUTTONHOLE OPENING

Reinforce the buttonhole area with fusible interfacing, then make two machine buttonholes in the outside of the garment before you complete and apply the casing (A). When the casing is complete, pull the drawstring through with a bodkin or a safety pin pinned through the drawstring and pushed and pulled along.

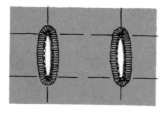

A

SEAM OPENINGS

Casing openings in a seam are made when you stitch the seam (B). For reinforcement, fuse a small rectangle of soft interfacing over the seamline on both sides of the opening. Then stitch your seam, leaving an opening where indicated on pattern tissue. When the casing is complete, the drawstring is inserted and pulled through in the same manner as for a buttonhole opening.

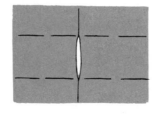

B

To keep ribbon drawstrings from fraying, coat the ends with clear nail polish.

To keep a drawstring from pulling out, center it exactly and then stitch through both the drawstring and casing at the center back. The drawstring will gather the sides and front equally, from the center back to the opening.

Facings

A facing is an edge finishing that conceals raw edges. Facings are used most frequently at garment openings such as armholes and necklines. A shaped facing, which is one that is cut to the shape of the garment area it finishes, usually is made of the same fabric as the garment.

Another kind of facing is a purchased bias binding, which can be used in place of a fabric facing.

Most easy patterns will instruct you to apply facings with a flat construction method, before garment side seams are stitched. This is an easier way to stitch, press and understitch because your garment goes through the machine flat and you don't have to worry about maneuvering stitched armhole or neckline circles under the presser foot.

SHAPED

1. *If your pattern has more than one facing section, first join the sections at their seamlines, aligning notches. The seamlines should meet and join perfectly at a curved section.*

2. Finish the outside edge of the facing according to the method most suitable for your garment, whether it's zigzag edging or a turned-under hem. See pages 167–168 for a review of seam finish options. Pin the facing to your garment, right sides together, and stitch.

   To eliminate bulk, grade the seam allowances, cutting the facing seam allowance narrower than the garment seam allowance. To do this easily, hold your scissors at an angle and cut both edges at once.

   Trim close to the stitching at any corner, and clip and/or notch almost to the stitching around curved areas. When you have finished grading, trimming and clipping, press the seam allowances open first, to obtain a sharp edge at the seam, and then toward the facing to form an even edge.

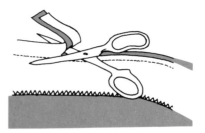

3. Turn the facing to the wrong side of the garment and press. Always favor the outside of the garment when you press by rolling the seam slightly toward the facing side. This keeps the facing from showing on the right side of your garment.

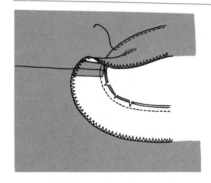

4. Even with proper pressing, facings can roll back to the right side. To reinforce the fold and hold the facing securely on the wrong side, understitch through the facing and the seam allowances. See page 90 for information on understitching.

5. Once you understitch the facing, it is unnecessary to then secure it all around the edge, but it is a good idea to secure it at the seams. Either tack it in place with a few stitches or apply a small piece of fusible web and press.

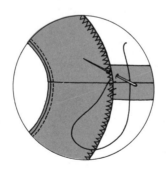
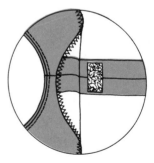

BIAS

Purchased double-fold bias tape makes a fast facing. It is sold in packages and is available in more and more fashion colors. It is also available in various widths.

1. *Open out one long edge of the bias tape.*
   Pin the right side of the tape to the right side of your garment edge, matching the crease line of the tape with the seamline of the garment, being careful not to stretch the tape. Turn the short ends up, to the wrong side, to form a finished edge when the tape is turned to the wrong side. Stitch along the crease line of the tape. Trim the seam allowance even with the edge of the tape, then clip through all thicknesses.

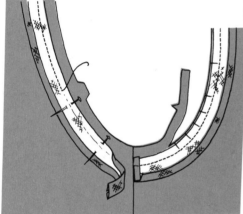

2. *Turn the bias tape to the wrong side, press and machine or hand stitch it in place all along the edge.*
   If using binding instead of facing, use flat construction methods to apply binding and then stitch seams, stitching through binding. Simply turn and finish binding.

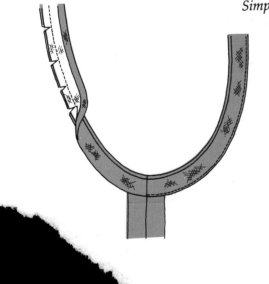

Hems

Hemlines go up and down with some regularity. Along with the changes in fashion trends have come some changes in hemming methods that have made the process of creating even, smooth hems an easy one. A hem is the raw edge of fabric at a sleeve, skirt, pant leg, blouse or jacket bottom that is finished, turned toward the inside of the garment and attached. The finishing methods vary widely, but one step that is the same for all types of hems is measuring and marking the length of the garment edges to be hemmed.

HEMLINE MARKING

Your pattern tells you two things about your hem. First, the pattern envelope lists the finished back length of the garment. Second, the pattern tissue or instruction sheet indicates how much of a hem allowance is provided. These are factors you take into consideration before you ever cut out your pattern, in case you have to make a length adjustment. The finished back length measurement plus the hem allowance is the actual top to bottom measurement for your garment. The amount of hem allowance provided and the style of the garment determine the type of hem that is the most suitable.

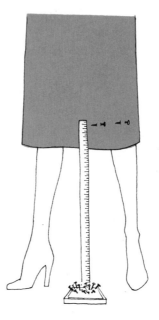

If no friend or chalk hem marker is available to help you measure your hem, tack a chalk-coated string across a doorway at the hem height you need. Gently move against it. The chalk will transfer to your skirt.

To save time when measuring a hem with a yardstick, put a rubber band around it at the correct hem length. The eyes of the person helping you measure focus right on the rubber band instead of searching for the small measuring line.

1. *Hemlines at your legs, whether skirts, dresses or pants, are measured from the floor up, preferably with the aid of another person. Wear the same type of undergarments and shoes wih the same heel height you will when wearing the finished garment. Also wear a belt or sash if one is part of how the garment will be worn, since that also affects the garment length. If you plan to wear the garment with a jacket, wear it during marking to check the proportions. Use a yardstick or a hem marker (see pages 22–23 for information on both) and, either with pins or tailor's chalk, mark all around where the bottom edge of the garment should be. If you use pins, insert them parallel to the floor. This mark creates the foldline for turning up the raw edge to the inside of the garment.*

Remove the garment, turn up the hem along the markings and pin it in place, inserting the pins perpendicular to the floor so the garment can fall naturally. Pins placed parallel to the hem at this point cause the garment to jut out or peak at the ends of the pins.

Try on the garment again to make sure the hem falls evenly and the length is as you want it to be.

For bias or circular skirts, however, it is necessary to let them hang for 24 hours before you mark the hem. This is because the bias angle of the fabric stretches it slightly, possibly requiring an adjustment to the hem to even it again.

Sometimes, even though the hem is straight, it can appear uneven either because of slight differences in your body from one side to the other or because of optical illusions in the fabric. If this is the case, adjust the hem until it looks even. For most garments, you can continue immediately with the next hemming step.

2. *Because seams add a structured dimension to your garment, trim to 1/4" (6mm) any seam allowances that cross the hem. This reduces bulk, helps make the seam a more equal weight to the rest of the garment and prevents ridges when the hem is pressed.*

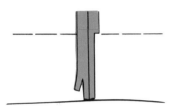

3. *Use the folded or bottom edge of the hem as a measuring guide to even the raw edge. Slight cutting or stitching differences can make this edge uneven. It should be as even as the bottom, so that when you finish it, it won't be bumpy or rippled. With a ruler or hem gauge, measure hem depth along the entire circumference, marking with*

chalk or a marking pen or pencil. Trim, if necessary, along the marks. Press the

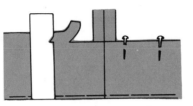

hem, inserting brown paper strips between the hem allowance and the garment. Baste along the hem fold and remove the pins. The raw edge now is prepared for finishing according to the method most suitable for your garment.

There are three particularly easy hem finishes that work on many types of garments. A narrow hem is not difficult because it requires very little easing, since there is not a great difference between the raw edge and the fold. A topstitched hem is easy because it is finished fast, by machine, and a fused hem because it requires no stitching at all.

NARROW HEM

1. *Turn up the hem along hemline and press. Trim the hem allowance to 3/8" or 5/8" (10cm or 15cm).*

   Turn under the raw edge until it touches the crease and press. Turn up on hemline and stitch.

2. *Since a narrow hem is topstitched, you may add a second row of topstitching if it is compatible with the look of the rest of your garment.*

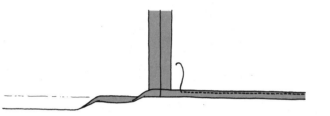

3. *If you have a narrow hemmer attachment for your sewing machine, folding and stitching is done in one step with this special foot. Guide the fabric by pre-folding it about 1" (25mm) in front of the foot as you stitch. This attachment works best on lightweight fabrics.*

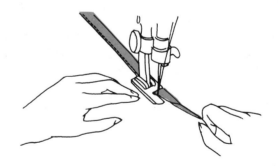

4. *To narrow-hem knit fabrics, turn up and press the hem allowance and stitch 1/4" (6mm) from the fold. Trim close to the stitching.*

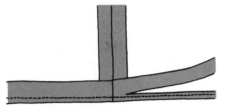

5. *For the narrowest hem of all, double knit and jersey fabrics may be zigzag stitched directly along the hemline. Use a small, narrow zigzag and trim away the hem allowance as close to the stitching as possible. This is a decorative stitch in addition to being an easy procedure and should be compatible with the fashion look of the rest of your garment.*

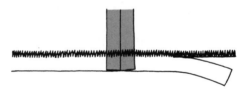

141

TOPSTITCHED HEMS

1. *If other areas of your garment are topstitched, the hem generally is topstitched at the same distance from the edge as they are, to keep a balanced look from top to bottom. Turn up the hem at the markings, matching seam allowances. Finish the raw edge in the manner most suitable for your fabric.*

2. *The hem is secured with one row of topstitching an even distance from the folded hem edge. More than one row, on a wider hem, can be a decorative addition to your garment. Use either matching or contrasting thread. If you are not making a narrow hem, measure the depth to be no more than 1" to 1-1/2" (25mm–3.8cm). Trim off any excess. Start your stitching at the folded hem edge. Space the topstitching rows approximately 1/4" (6mm) apart. As with any other topstitching, it is important that the stitching lines be straight and parallel. Use the toe of your presser foot as a stitching guide, lining up the first row of stitching on the right side of the right toe.*

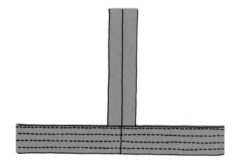

FUSED HEMS

1. *Fusing is a very fast way to complete a hem. As with any other garment section you fuse, it is important to complete all measuring, trimming and pressing steps before applying the fusible web. Even the hem depth, finish the raw edge and press, using brown paper strips between the hem allowance and the garment.*

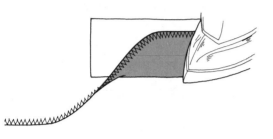

2. *Strips of fusible web, rather than patches, ensure a smooth finish. Cut strips or use pre-cut web to fit around the circumference of your hem. Position the web about 1/4" (6mm) below the hem edge. This placement prevents the hem edge from showing through to the right side of the garment and keeps the web away from the soleplate of your iron. See page 78 for fusing directions and for tips on removing web in case you need to make a hem alteration.*

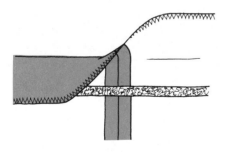

143

Hooks and Eyes

There are several kinds of hooks and eyes, each designed to work with different fabric weights and at various stress points. Many come with either straight eyes, used for lapped edges or curved eyes, used for edges that meet. They are nickel or finished in black enamel, and range in size from fine (0) to heavy (3).

COVERED

Covered hook and eye sets usually are larger and are particularly good for closing coats and garments of heavier fabrics. They have loop, rather than straight, eyes.

WAISTBAND

Waistband hooks and eyes are very sturdy and are designed to keep the hook on skirts and pants, where there is strain on the closure, securely fastened. They are available in nickel or black finish.

APPLYING HOOKS AND EYES TO EDGES THAT MEET

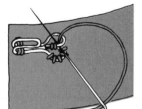

When closing edges meet but do not overlap, use a hook and curved eye.

1. *Sew them to the wrong side of the garment with the hook 1/16" (2mm) from one edge and the loop of the eye positioned slightly beyond the other edge.*

2. *Sew around each hole and sew around the end of the hook and the eye to secure them and hold them flat.*

APPLYING HOOKS AND EYES TO EDGES THAT OVERLAP

When edges overlap, as on skirts and pants, use two hooks with straight eyes or a waistband hook and eye.

1. *Place the hook on the side that will be overlapped, about 1/4"
(6mm) from the edge.*

2. *Mark the position of the eye on the inside of the overlap with pins,
positioning the pins where the end of the hook lines up.*

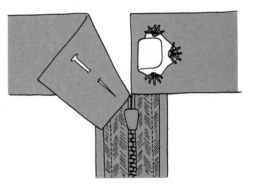

3. *Sew through all the holes to make the hook secure. Stitching should
not show on right side.*

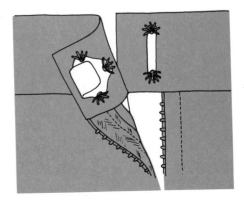

145

Nylon Hook and Loop Tape

Nylon hook and loop tape, most commonly known as Velcro, is an easy closure that can be used in many sections of a loose-fitting garment and for home decorating accessories, often in place of zippers, hooks and eyes, snaps and buttons. Nylon tape should not be used on tight-fitting garments or with very lightweight fabrics when the tapes would be bulkier and heavier than the fabric.

It consists of two tapes; one portion is the hook side, the other is the loop side, which is fuzzy in appearance. Since the hook side is rough, always position it away from the body to avoid skin irritation. When pressed together, the hooks and loops lock. To separate them, just pull them apart. Nylon tapes are available in various widths, colors and weights and can be purchased by the yard and in pre-cut packages for a closure on a long garment section, and in dots, circles and squares for a spot closure such as at a neckline or cuff. Some tapes are self-basting: They are made with adhesive on the wrong side for easy placement. If the tape you choose is not self-basting, hold the tapes in position for stitching with pins or with basting tape across the center, or use a glue stick.

1. *The garment edges or seam allowance should be wider than the tapes to prevent tape edges from showing when the garment is closed. Place the hook tape on the underlap and stitch around all the edges, through all layers of fabric.*

2. *Align the loop side of the tape on the overlap. To make sure both sides are aligned, close the garment the way it is to be worn, trying it on, if possible, and mark the placement lines.*

3. *After the loop tape is aligned on the overlap, stitch around all sides close to the edges, through all layers of fabric. When washing garments with hook and loop tape, always close the tape to prevent the hook side from snagging other garments.*

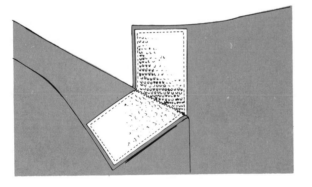

Pockets

Without a doubt, pockets are designed for a purpose. Prominently placed and beautifully stitched, patch pockets can add a decorative touch to a garment. Pockets can be practical, too. For example, pockets are a good place to store your keys, put your hands or tuck a tissue. If you are apprehensive every time a garment requires a pocket—especially on a very visible part of your garment—read on and discover some easy ways to create pocket perfection.

PATCH POCKETS

Patch pockets are applied *to* a garment. They most often are placed on blouse and jacket fronts, on skirts and on pants as back pockets.

When positioning patch pockets on a garment, be sure the pockets flatter you. For example, if you are full-busted, omitting large pockets at the bust on blouses, dresses and jackets might do more for you than the pockets will do for the garment!

Before cutting out or stitching a patch pocket, be sure that one-way designs, like flowers, are "growing" in the right direction. For nap fabrics, like corduroy, be sure that the pocket's nap runs in the same direction as the nap of the garment piece to which it will be attached.

If a pair of pockets is to be placed on your garment, be sure they are cut, finished and sewn identically.

Unlined Patch Pockets—
Square

1. *To be sure that the top pocket edge is even, transfer the pattern foldline from the pattern to the pocket piece with chalk, marking pen or pencil. See page 56 for marking techniques.*

   To finish the upper edge, use the method most appropriate for your fabric. Create a pocket facing by folding the top edge to the right side of the pocket, along the foldline. Press along the fold.

   Stitch around the pocket just inside the seamline in the seam allowance. Trim only the facing seam allowance.

2. *Turn the facing to the inside. If necessary, use a pointer and creaser to carefully push out the corners of the pocket so that they are neatly squared. Press the facing in place.*

   On the remaining edges, turn the seam allowances to the inside. Press, rolling the stitching lines to the inside. Miter the bottom corners to make them smooth and sharp. See pages 124–125 for mitering techniques.

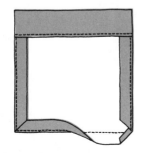

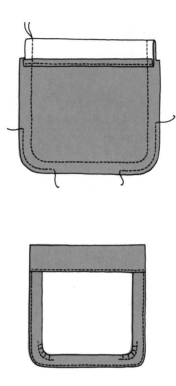

Rounded

1. *When you want rounded instead of square-bottom corners prepare your pockets as in step 1 above.*

   Easestitch along each curve in the seam allowance, 1/4" (6mm) from the cut edge. Turn the facing to the wrong side of the pocket, square the upper corners and press.

2. *As you turn under the seam allowance for pressing along the stitching lines, be sure to gently roll the stitches away from the pocket front so that the stitches do not show on the right side.*

   Ease the pocket curves into shape by carefully pulling the bobbin thread and adjusting the gathers. If there is too much bulk from the gathers, clip notches in the seam allowance at the curves. Press.

For perfectly even pockets every time, make or purchase a template for the size square or rounded pocket you make most often. To use, simply press your pockets over the template.

Lined Patch Pockets

Generally, patch pockets are unlined, with the foldover facing at the top finishing the top edge. However, occasionally it is desirable to use a lightweight lining in the construction.

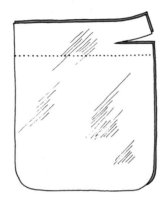

1. *Line a patch pocket to the edge by cutting out one pocket piece from the fabric and one identical pocket piece from the lining. Mark the top edge foldline on the lining piece and trim both pieces 5/8" (15mm) above the foldline. This becomes the seam allowance when you stitch the two layers together.*

2. *Stitch the lining to the pocket along the seamline on all sides, but leave an opening at the bottom large enough for turning. Trim the seam allowances.*

   For a smooth, square corner, make a diagonal cut across the seam allowance just beyond the point where the stitching turns.

   For a well-rounded edge, notch the excess fabric around the outside curves so that the curve will lie flat.

   Turn the pocket right side out. Smooth the round edges. If necessary, push out square corners with a pointer and creaser. As you press the pocket, carefully roll the lining toward the pocket back, so that the lining won't show on the pocket side. Slipstitch the opening closed.

Here's a quick method for turning lined patch pockets. After stitching around the entire pocket and lining, sewn right sides together, make a slash in the lining near the bottom edge. Pull the pocket through the slash. Fuse a small piece of interfacing to close the slash.

Applying Patch Pockets

Make sure your garment pieces are properly marked before applying patch pockets. When it comes to decorative patch pockets, placement and appearance are everything.

If you have made pattern adjustments in the length of your garment, recheck the pocket placement before applying the pocket on the main pattern piece. If you don't and follow the pattern's original pocket placement instead, you could end up with a pocket in an awkward position . . . and who needs a pocket under the arm! If you plan to *use* patch pockets that fall below your waist, be sure they are in a comfortable position for you to reach. Pockets that are too low or too high are unusable.

If your pattern markings are on the wrong side of your garment sections, carefully transfer these markings to the right side of your garment piece so you know exactly where to place your pocket or pockets. This can be done easily and accurately by sticking a pin through the piece from the wrong side, where the marking is, to the right side where it should be.

A patch pocket can be applied to a garment visibly or invisibly, once the markings are transferred. There are several methods from which to select. For the easiest construction, apply pockets to a flat garment piece whenever possible.

For topstitching spaced a wide distance from the first row and to keep it even, use sewing or transparent tape as your stitching guide. Once the pocket is secured on the garment, determine the distance you would like the topstitching to be and place the tape on the pocket, parallel to the pocket edges. Be sure that one tape edge measures the right distance from the pocket edge. Keep your needle close to the tape edge as you stitch around the sides and bottom of the pocket.

1. *Before a pocket is permanently stitched, secure it to the garment. Either baste it in place by machine, hand or with pins, or fuse it in place by*

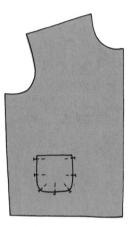

aligning three narrow strips of fusible web directly under the side and bottom edges so they don't show. See page 78 for fusible web techniques. You also can glue the pocket in place with a glue stick. Apply a thin film of glue along the seam allowance at the side and bottom edges of the pocket, then turn the pocket over and finger press it directly on the garment at the pocket markings.

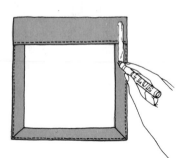

2. *After securing the pocket, you may edgestitch and/or topstitch it, if compatible with the edge finishes on the rest of your garment. First, reinforce the top edges of your pocket to keep them from pulling out during wear. Machine backstitch at each top corner and then edgestitch and/or topstitch the pocket from the top of one pocket edge down and around to the top of the other pocket edge.*

To create a double topstitched effect, use your presser foot as a guide to topstitch an equal distance from the first row of stitches around the pocket again.

3. *To attach your pockets invisibly, carefully secure them in place on the outside of the garment piece and sew them, by hand, along the pocket edge from the inside of the garment. It helps to have your markings on the inside as well as on the outside so that you are sure to catch the pocket as you sew. Be careful that your stitches don't go through the pocket.*

A clever way to be sure your topstitching comes out evenly, without having to worry about joining the pocket to the garment at the same time, is to prepare the pocket for stitching and topstitch the pocket by itself. After topstitching, place the pocket on the garment, secure it and, using the presser foot or tape as your stitching guide, edgestitch it in place.

153

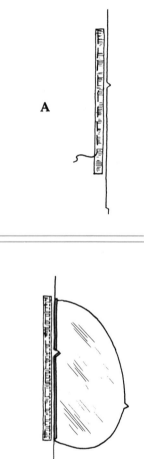

A

B

IN-SEAM POCKETS

In-seam pockets are very handy. They are found in skirts, pants and dresses. Properly constructed, these pockets should be practically undetectable. One of the ways to accomplish this is to use lightweight lining fabric.

Because an in-seam pocket does get a lot of use and stress, it is worth the effort—small though it is—to construct a stay that will reinforce the pocket edge and help protect it from stretching.

1. *You can easily construct a pocket stay with a piece of ribbon seam binding cut 2" (5cm) longer than the pocket opening. Place the garment front wrong side up and center the seam binding on the seamline at the pocket opening. Machine baste in place (A).*

2. *Join the pocket pieces to their corresponding front and back garment sections. For each section, place the right sides of garment fabric together, match pocket markings and stitch a 1/4" (6mm) seam. Fold the pockets across the stitching and press on the wrong side (B).*

3. *With right sides together, baste the garment fronts to the garment backs.*

    To permanently stitch the pieces together, begin stitching at the lower seam and continue around the pocket to the upper seam. You can maintain an even seam allowance by pivoting at the points where the seamline turns at the pocket. These points are marked on your pattern (C).

4. *To make the seams lie flat, pull the pocket toward the garment front and clip only the back seam allowance just above and below the pocket. Press the seam open above and below the pocket (D).*

C

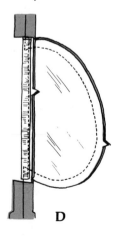

D

SIDE FRONT POCKETS

Side front pockets are attached to a garment at the waist and side seams. Therefore, the same adjustments made at the waist or side seamline, if any, must also be made on the side front pocket pieces before construction.

Unlike in-seam pockets, side front pockets are made up of two entirely different pattern piece shapes. One piece is called the side front section because it is attached to the garment at the waist and side seamline. The side front section almost always is cut from self fabric, because it eventually becomes an integral and visible part of the garment. The other piece, the pocket section, is more like a facing. Because it remains unseen, the pocket section can be cut from either self fabric or lining fabric.

The pocket opening of a side front pocket is cut on the bias and is very susceptible to stretching. An easy-to-assemble reinforcing stay prevents such stretching and keeps your side front pockets in good shape.

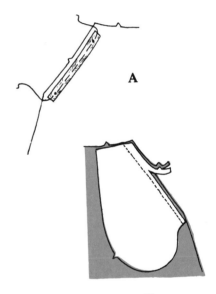

A

B

1. *Cut a piece of ribbon seam binding 2" (5cm) longer than the pocket opening. Place the garment front wrong side up and center the seam binding on the seamline at the pocket opening. Machine baste in place (A).*

   Pin the pocket section to the corresponding slanted edge of the garment front, matching notches, and stitch in place along the seamline. Trim the seam to 1/4" (6mm) (B).

2. *Pull the pocket to the inside of the garment and press the pocket edge down. To prevent the pocket from rolling outward, carefully understitch through the pocket and seam allowance, keeping as close to the seamline as possible (C).*

   You also can prevent the pocket from rolling by topstitching along the pocket's finished edge.

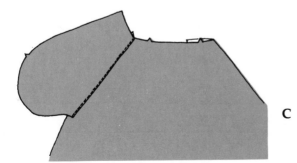

C

3. *With right sides together, match notches and pin the side front section to the pocket section. Stitch around the pocket seamline from the side seam to the waist. Only stitch on the notched side of the pockets—do* not *stitch up the pocket opening! You can finish the raw pocket edges with zigzag stitches or you can cut along the pocket edge with pinking shears.*

4. *Turn the pocket inside the garment and baste it to the garment front where it meets at the waist area and the side edges.*

After completing the side front pocket construction, proceed with the regular garment construction by joining the front and back sections at the sides. Be sure that when you stitch the waistline seam you treat the upper edge of the pocket as part of the upper edge of the garment.

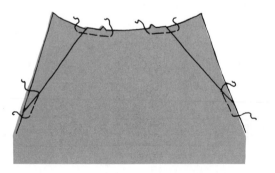

Ruffles

If you get ruffled at the thought of sewing ruffles, keep these pointers in mind. Although a ruffle seems like a lot of fabric to deal with, it is not at all difficult to bring it quickly to a manageable size and apply it to your garment for a soft fashion touch. An easy, straight ruffle begins as a straight strip of fabric that is at least twice as long as the garment section to which it is attached. When it is gathered, the fullness becomes ruffled and the strip is drawn to the same size as the garment section. Soft, lightweight fabrics are the easiest to ruffle and have the best finished appearance.

Your pattern piece for a ruffle often indicates that you are to cut from two or more layers of fabric. Make sure they match each other in pattern and grain direction. Easy patterns call for straight ruffles cut either on the straight or crosswise grain. When the strips are stitched together at the short ends, they form one long strip. Seam them right sides together and press the seam allowances open.

Two easy straight ruffles are single ruffles, which have a narrow hem finish, and double ruffles, which are made from a strip of fabric twice the width of the finished ruffle plus seam allowances. Which you choose depends on the finished look you desire. Double ruffles are faster and easier to construct, since you do not need to finish the hem edge.

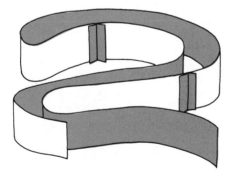

SINGLE

1. *This kind of plain ruffle can be whatever width your pattern calls for or that you prefer. Narrow hem the ruffle to the hem width recommended on the pattern before it is gathered. Gather the unfinished edge. To prepare for gathering, stitch one row of long machine stitches at the seamline of the unfinished long edge and a second row 1/4" (6mm) from the first, in the seam allowance. One row of gathering stitches works, but the second row serves as a timesaver: In case the thread breaks on the first row, the second can be gathered immediately without the need for restitching. Having two rows of gathering stitches also helps control and direct the fullness. See pages 85–87 for more information on gathering.*

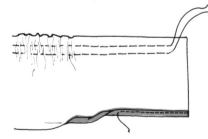

2. *To apply a single ruffle to a garment edge, pin the ruffle strip to the garment right sides together, matching ends and seams. Pull the bobbin thread to gather, and adjust the gathers until they are evenly distributed, securing the other end of the thread by wrapping it in a figure eight around a pin. Pin baste or machine baste in place. Gather the ruffle to fit and machine stitch it in place.*

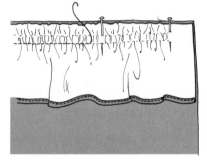

3. *Trim the seam allowance to 3/8" (10mm). Press ruffle seam allowance flat and then toward garment. If desired topstitch along the edge, through the seam allowances.*

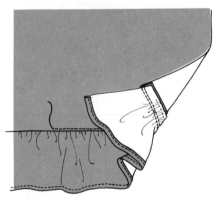

DOUBLE

This kind of ruffle is made by folding a single strip of fabric in half, wrong sides together. This procedure automatically gives a finished edge to the bottom of the ruffle.

1. *Fold and press the strip. Stitch gathering rows, the first at the seamline and the second 1/4" (6mm) away, in the seam allowance.*

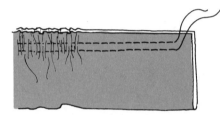

2. *To apply the ruffle to a garment edge, follow the same procedure as for a single-layer ruffle, pinning the ruffle strip to the garment, right sides together, matching ends and the seamlines.*

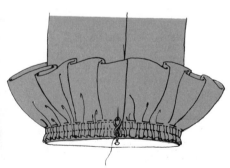

3. *Press the seam allowances, being careful not to press into the ruffle. This could set in unwanted creases or wrinkles.*

RUFFLES IN A SEAM

1. *When either a single ruffle or a double ruffle is to be enclosed in a seam, pin it to the garment, right sides together, adjust the gathers and smooth the ruffle, making sure only the ruffle seam allowance is caught in the seam.*

   Stitch the ruffle to secure it, 1/8" (3mm) away from the stitching line, within the seam allowance. Remove all pins.

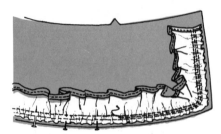

2. *Pin the garment section with the attached ruffle to the second garment section so the ruffle is sandwiched between the right sides of both sections.*

   Stitch on the seamline. Trim, grade and clip edges and corners to eliminate bulk along the stitching and turn the garment section to the right side. Finish the garment edge according to pattern directions.

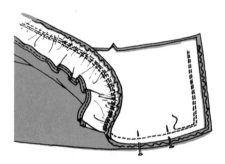

Seams

Seams deserve a lot more respect than they often get. Don't ever let anyone tell you that a seam is *just* a line of stitching that joins two pieces of fabric together. In most cases, without at least one seam, there is no garment. But, more important, without a well-constructed seam, there is a misshapen mess! Even though you can't (or shouldn't) *see* the seam stitching itself, poor seam habits have a way of making themselves known.

Puckers and pulls are just two of the many ailments that can result from a badly made seam, and ailments like these can often spell disaster for an entire sewing project. Why suffer through all that? Since the cure *is* so easy, it really does pay to concentrate on constructing the *best* seam you possibly can. Not only will your efforts save you enormous amounts of time and tension, your well-made seams will reward you with a beautifully constructed garment.

In order to prevent time-consuming seam rip-outs, get in the habit of stitching a test seam on some scraps of garment fabric, with the thread you intend to use, before you begin joining pattern pieces. Sew through two thicknesses of fabric, leaving a seam allowance—the fabric between the seamline and the cut edge—just as you would sew a seam.

If your seams pucker, your sewing machine could be the culprit. Maybe the machine tension on the bobbin or needle thread is too loose or too tight, or maybe the pressure on the presser foot isn't right. See page 82 for how to adjust machine tension and pressure.

STRAIGHT STITCHED SEAMS

A straight stitched seam is constructed with one row of stitching. Don't let the name mislead you; straight stitched seams can be applied to curved and angled areas as well.

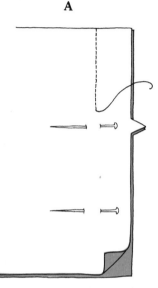

A

1. *Place right sides of fabric pieces together, match notches and markings and position pins securely at right angles along the fabric edge. Keep the pin heads in the seam allowance so that you can remove them easily as you sew.*

   For a simple seam, pin basting the pieces together should be enough to hold them firmly in place for accurate stitching (A). See pages 57–59 for more on basting techniques.

   An alternative method for holding fabric layers together is using basting tape or double-faced tape. Be sure to test the tape on some garment fabric scraps to see if the tape holds the layers firmly in place as you sew, and be sure that the tape won't hurt the fabric surface in any way. To use the tape, place it in the seam allowance, 1/4" away from the seamline, so you don't stitch through the tape as you sew. Remove the tape before pressing (B).

2. *After determining the direction in which you must stitch the seam so that you keep it with the grain, place the piece to be seamed under the presser foot with the seam allowance to the right of the presser foot and the rest of the piece to the left of the presser foot. Lower the needle so that it falls on the seamline. Seamlines usually are 5/8" (15mm) from the cut edge, but they sometimes are narrower. Always double check your pattern for seam width before you sew. To prevent your fabric from pulling into the needle plate, put your needle into the fabric 1/2" (13mm) from the top edge, then lower the presser foot. Backstitch to the edge before stitching the length of the seam (C). To reinforce the other end of the seam, set the machine to stitch backward, and backstitch a 1/2" (13mm) up from the end, right over the seam stitches.*

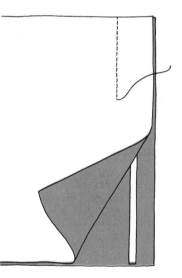

B

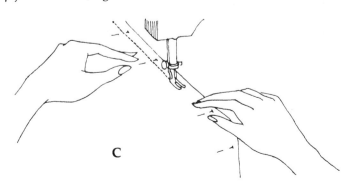

C

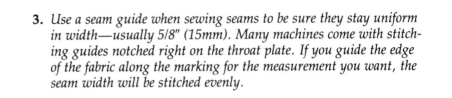

3. *Use a seam guide when sewing seams to be sure they stay uniform in width—usually 5/8" (15mm). Many machines come with stitching guides notched right on the throat plate. If you guide the edge of the fabric along the marking for the measurement you want, the seam width will be stitched evenly.*

Some machines come with a seam guide attachment that can be adjusted to different seam widths. This attachment is particularly useful on curved seams.

You can make your own seam guide by placing a piece of tape (like masking or adhesive) to the right of the presser foot on the throat plate, so it runs parallel to the presser foot. Just be sure that the distance from one of the tape edges to the center of the needle measures the desired width.

A quick assembly-line trick that helps you get all your seams sewn as efficiently as possible is continuous stitching. It not only hastens your seam-sewing time, it also prevents you from losing any of the pieces—because they're all attached! Pin or baste together all the pieces that need to be seamed. Stitch each seam, but instead of cutting the threads when you finish the seam, draw out a piece of thread from the needle and bobbin that is long enough to let you move the piece you just seamed out of the way. Then you can stitch the next seam. Proceed with each seam in the same manner. You end up with a long string of seamed pieces tethered by uncut thread. After you've finished all the seam stitching, press each seam. When you're ready to assemble the garment, simply snip the threads and sew.

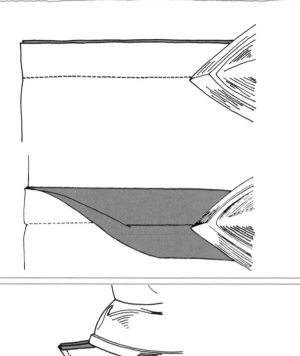

Pressing Seams

1. *Press the stitching line flat so that the stitches blend into the fabric, then press the seam open.*

2. *You can get a good sharp point on enclosed seams in collars and cuffs by pressing them open with a point presser.*

Trimming Seams

1. *Seam allowances are trimmed to eliminate bulk. Enclosed seam allowances, like those in collars and cuffs, are trimmed to 1/4" (6mm). Cut the corners diagonally at the seam ends, particularly if the seam eventually crosses another seam.*

2. *To make sure that corners on enclosed seams, such as those on collars and cuffs, turn out to be as sharp as possible, first cut straight across the point at the stitches and then trim the seam allowances at an angle along either side of the point.*

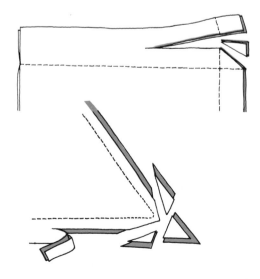

163

Grading Seams

To maintain the sleek look of a garment, it is essential that all seams lie as flat as possible. Often it is necessary to grade, or gradually trim, the seam allowance so that it is smooth and unnoticeable from the right side. Each layer should be trimmed a different width, with the garment seam allowance the widest and applied sections narrower. Enclosed seams on collars and cuffs generally are trimmed narrower than exposed seams in necklines and front closings that have facings.

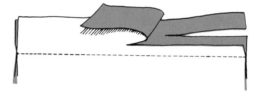

Notching and Clipping on Curved Seams

Curved seams must be graded, pressed and then notched or clipped to lie flat. Very carefully, with your scissors, cut into the seam allowance, clipping inside curves and notching outside curves. The clips should be spaced approximately 1/2" to 1" apart (13mm to 25mm), depending on the sharpness of the curve. The sharper the curve, the closer the clips.

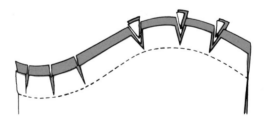

If, by mistake, you trim a seam too close to the stitches, dab a commercial product like Fray Check or some clear nail polish along the seam allowance to prevent the fabric from pulling away from the stitching.

TOPSTITCHED SEAMS

Be inventive, be creative . . . and add your very own decorative touch with topstitched seams. It's actually stitching done on the surface of the garment, right after the seam is stitched so that the pieces are flat and easy to handle. You can introduce an interesting new design element to a tailored garment just by changing the thread color. Solid fabrics and lightly patterned prints are the perfect vehicles for topstitched seams.

1. *A single-topstitched seam has one row of stitching running parallel to the main seam stitching. It can be decorative only, or it can be a finishing technique for fabric edges and hems. After stitching the seam, press both seam allowances to the side you plan to topstitch. Add a row of topstitching 1/4" (6mm) from the seam on the right side.*

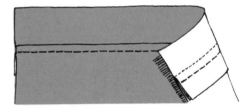

2. *For double-topstitched seams, construct a straight-stitched seam and press the seam allowances open. With the right side of your fabric facing up, topstitch either 1/8" (3mm) or 1/4" (6mm) on both sides of the seamline, using the seamline as your stitching guide. Be sure you're sewing through each seam allowance on the underside as you stitch.*

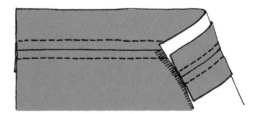

165

MOCK FLAT-FELLED SEAMS

You easily can create the look of a more intricately constructed flat-felled seam with a mock flat-felled seam. The major dif-ference between the two meth-ods is that the mock version leaves a raw edge on the seam allowance.

1. *With right sides together, construct a straight-stitched seam. Press the seam allowances open, then press them to the side on which you want the second row of stitching.*

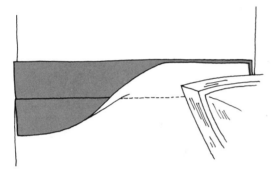

2. *On the right side of the garment section, edgestitch next to the seam, then topstitch 1/4" (6mm) from the seam, through the seam allowances. Use the straight-stitched seam as a guide for topstitching. Trim the seam allowances close to the topstitching.*

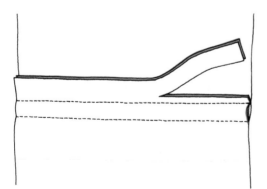

Seam Finishes

Even though you can't see it while you're wearing the garment, a neat seam finish not only is esthetically pleasing as you take the garment off or put it on, it also can give the garment a longer life by making the seams more durable.

PINKED AND STITCHED

This finish works well for fabrics that don't ravel badly and for heavy fabrics because it does not add bulk.

After the seam is stitched and pressed open stitch along the length of the seam allowance, 1/4" (6mm) from each raw edge. Pink the edge of each seam allowance with pinking shears.

TURNED AND STITCHED

This finish is also called the clean finish, because it brings a neat, clean, tailored finish to light and medium-weight fabrics. The turned and stitched method also can be used to finish unlined jackets if the fabric is not too bulky.

With right sides together, construct a straight-stitched seam. Press the seam allowances open. Turn both raw edges of the seam allowances under 1/4" (6mm).

Fold back your garment section and edgestitch along the fold on the seam allowance edges only, taking care to catch the edge underneath as you stitch.

If your fabric is hard to handle and you find it difficult to maneuver the stitching and raw edges at the same time, an easy solution is to first run a stitch line along each seam allowance 1/4" (6mm) from each edge. This becomes a foldline and guide, making it easy to turn the fabric. Fold and press the edge under at the stitching line and edgestitch along the fold.

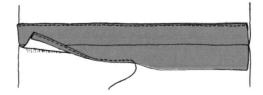

MACHINE ZIGZAG

This is a good finish for fabrics that tend to ravel easily. Use narrow stitches for lightweight

fabrics and wider stitches for bulky fabrics. It's a good idea to pre-test this finish on fabric scraps to be sure the stitch length and width are correct. Once you have determined the correct length and width, stitch close to the raw edge, with the zigzag points stopping just short of the edge.

APPLIED SEAM

Applied seam finishes give a neat, professional look to seams that are sure to be seen, such as in an unlined coat or jacket. They also are useful on seam edges that ravel.

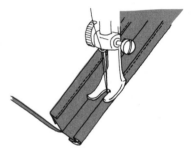

With right sides together, construct a straight-stitched seam. Press the seam allowances open. Trim any notches from the seam edge. Measure two strips of double-fold bias tape equal to the length of the seam edges that are to be bound. Place the wider side of the tape under the raw edge of the seam and fold the narrower side over the edge. To hold the tape in place for stitching, place pins at right angles to the seam edge. Stitch along the narrow side of the bias tape, through the seam allowance only, taking care to catch the wider side underneath as you stitch. Repeat the procedure for the other seam allowance.

Besides double-fold bias tape for applied seam finishes, there

is now a very lightweight sheer bias binding available for use on all types of fabrics. These bindings finish seam edges and keep them from raveling, but because they are sheer, they do not conceal them. If you use them on the inside seams of unlined jackets and coats, keep in mind that the raw edges still show. These bindings come in 5/8" (15mm) and 1-1/4" (3.2cm) widths, and work extremely well on curved seams because they are so flexible. They are not pre-folded, so you must determine the fold by slightly stretching the binding as you apply it.

To create finished edges on the inside of an unlined coat, sew it inside out! Stitch seams with garment pieces wrong sides together, so the inside has no raw edges. Trim the seam allowances to 1/4" (6mm) and conceal the raw edges, which are on the right side of the garment, by centering braid over the seam and pinning it in place with pins at right angles to the braid edges. Edgestitch along each braid edge.

Use Fray Check to finish raw edges. Lay your seam allowances on a flat, absorbant surface. Place Fray Check along each cut edge. This flat and easy method to finish seams also works well to repair small snags or tears in fabrics.

Sleeves

It's one thing to have a chip on your shoulder but quite another to have a bump, lump, pucker or wrinkle. The former goes away with time but the latter never do—it makes much more sense not to stitch them in in the first place! Constructing pucker-free sleeves is not difficult if you follow basic seam construction and pressing techniques to the letter.

Sleeves, in addition to having a professional finished appearance, should be comfortable. They shouldn't strain at the seams when you wear them. The two primary action areas of a sleeve correspond to the action of your arm at the elbow and the upper arm.

There are three basic types of sleeves. A set-in sleeve joins the garment at the shoulder in a seam that encircles the arm. The top of the sleeve is called the sleeve cap.

A raglan sleeve has diagonal seams that join it to the garment from the bodice front and back to the neckline area.

A kimono or dolman sleeve is cut as part of the bodice or yoke and seamed under the arm and at the shoulder along the top of the arm.

Which you choose is a matter of fashion preference. Try on various styles in ready-to-wear garments to see which are the most flattering to you before purchasing a pattern. Remember that raglan, kimono and dolman sleeves are faster and easier to construct than standard set-in sleeves and that set-in sleeves on a dropped-shoulder style have a flat sleeve cap, which is also easy to construct. Generally, sleeves are completed as a unit and then sewn into the garment after the side seams are sewn. Your instruction sheet gives you specific directions for this sleeve application.

Easy patterns try, whenever possible, to feature flat construction techniques for sleeves because they can be stitched much more easily when a garment is flat than when the major seams are already stitched.

SET-IN

RAGLAN

KIMONO

169

SET-IN

1. *Finish the hem edge of the sleeve before beginning the sleeve cap or shoulder construction using the method most suitable to your fabric.*

2. *Stitch the garment shoulder seams but leave the side seams open. Gather or easestitch the sleeve cap between the notches, using two rows of stitches. Stitch once at the seamline and again 1/4" (6mm) in the seam allowance. Pin the sleeve cap to the armhole edge and adjust the gathers, then steam press to shrink excess fullness. With the sleeve side facing you, machine stitch along the seamline and again 1/4" (6mm) away in the seam allowance to secure the sleeve to the garment.*

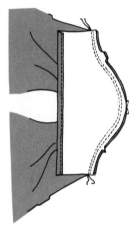

3. *Press the seam, first as it was stitched and then toward the sleeve. Clip the underarm curve.*

Pin the side seams and stitch the side of the garment and through the lower edge of the sleeve. Clip at the angle formed under the arm and press the seam open.

When attaching shoulder pads to a shoulder seam, stitch a strip of nylon hook and loop tape in position at the garment seam and one on top of the shoulder pad. This is an easy way to remove shoulder pads for laundering and pressing. Be sure to attach the loop section to the garment so the hook won't snag other garments while in the laundry.

RAGLAN

1. Finish the hem edge of the sleeve using the method most suitable to your fabric.

2. Pin the diagonal edges of the sleeve to the garment front and back, right sides together, matching symbols. Stitch along the seamlines. Trim and clip the seam allowances between the notches, at the underarm.

3. Press the seam open and stitch the garment side seams and the sleeve seam as one seam. Clip the angle formed under the arm. Press the seam open.

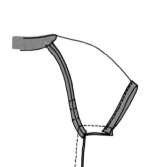

KIMONO

1. *Pin the garment front and back bodice pieces together, matching markings, and stitch along the seamline.*

Reinforce the underarm curve with a second row of small stitches, approximately 15 or 20 per inch (per 25mm). Since this seam area undergoes considerable wearing stress, the reinforcement keeps it from ripping.

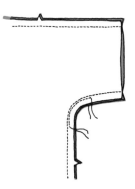

2. *Clip along the reinforced stitching to allow the curved area natural movement when you move your arm.*

Press the seam open over a press mitt or tailor's ham. See page 61 for pressing tips.

3. *Finish the hem edge of the sleeve using the method most compatible with your fabric.*

Sleeve Finishes

Often narrow sleeves have openings or fold-over pleat fastenings at the bottom edge. These lower-edge openings are for fit and wearing ease. There are three easy ways to create openings—by stitching a dart, by opening a seam and by narrow hemming. You also can fold the sleeve over at the hem and add two buttonholes and a button.

DART OPENING

1. *Stitch the dart in the lower edge following pattern markings. Slash to the pattern marking.*

2. *Roll the raw edges of the opening to the wrong side of the garment and press them flat.*

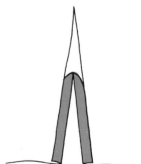

3. *Turn the raw edges under to finish them, and edgestitch or slip-stitch them to the garment.*

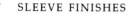

SEAM OPENING

1. *To create a seam opening, end seam stitching at the pattern markings, backstitching for reinforcement (A). Press the seam open.*

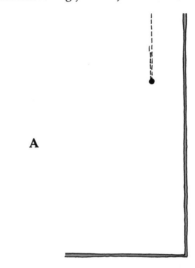

A

2. *Fold the raw edges in the sleeve opening as for a narrow hem (see page 140), tapering to nothing above pattern symbol. Press them in place (B).*

3. *Edgestitch along the edges and across the top of the opening (C).*

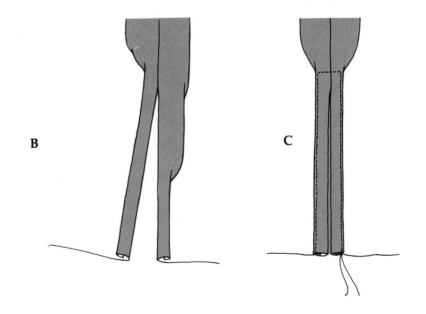

B

C

NARROW HEM
OPENING

1. To create a narrow hem opening, which is a wider finish than a dart or seam opening, reinforce the lower edge of the sleeve through pattern markings and clip to each marking.

2. Narrow hem the seam allowance and press.

PLEAT OPENING

1. After the bottom edge of the sleeve is finished, machine stitch two buttonholes at the markings, making sure they are exactly parallel and spaced so that when the fabric is folded vertically between them, they align. Sew a button to the sleeve edge at the marking. To check button placement, align the two buttonholes and bring the pleat to the button marking, making sure it is straight and doesn't strain or pull the fabric out of line.

2. Form the pleat as you button the sleeve edge by aligning the two buttonholes and folding them to the button.

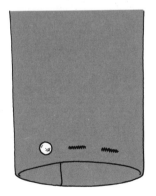
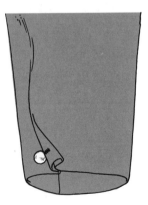

Snaps

There are many kinds of snaps available today, from sew-on snaps in metal or nylon and covered snaps to the newer, fast-method snap tapes and gripper snaps that do not require sewing. Snaps range in size from fine (4/0) to heavy (4) and are best used on overlapping edges that receive a minimum of strain, since they have less holding power than hooks and eyes. Each snap has a ball half with an extended ball in the center and a socket half with an indented center to receive the ball.

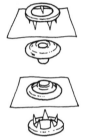

NO-SEW SNAPS

No-sew snaps are just that—snaps that require no sewing because they are cleated into the fabric instead. They do, however, require a tool for attaching them. There are several types from which to choose, three of which are illustrated here.

1. *Each snap to be attached comes in four parts—two parts for the ball side and two parts for the socket side. The tool presses each part together when they are positioned, one on the right side of your fabric, one on the wrong side.*

   These snaps come in different sizes. Select them according to the weight of your fabric. Too heavy a snap could pull right through fabric that isn't strong enough to support it. To give extra support, add one or two layers of interfacing between the garment and the seam allowance or facing.

2. *No-sew snaps are positioned the same way as are sew-on snaps, with the ball half attached first, on the underside of the overlap, far enough from the edge so it will not show. Position the socket half on the underlap to align with the ball.*

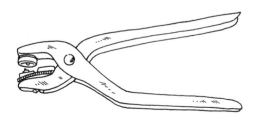

SNAP TAPE

Snap tape may be used only on edges that overlap and is a particularly easy way to apply snaps to infants' clothing and to casual sportswear jackets and shirts. The garment edges or seam allowance must be wider than the tape, so the tape edge won't extend over the fabric edge and show on the right side of your fabric.

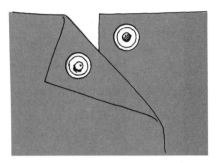

- *Position the socket tape on the underlap and stitch around the edges of all sides, through all layers. Align and position the ball tape on the underside or seam allowance of the overlap and stitch around the edges of all sides, through all layers.*

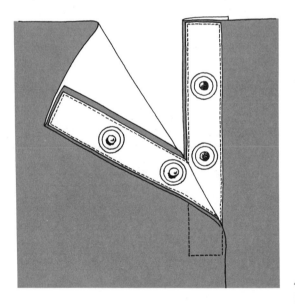

To line up no-sew snaps in a snap, rub the ball with tailor's chalk after it is attached, and press it onto the underlap. The transferred chalk mark is your guide for positioning the center of the socket.

177

Trims

One of the most fun sections to browse through in any fabric or notions store is the trims department. From absolutely elegant to ethnic to simple decoratives, trims are fascinating. As technology improves, the availability of such things as laces that look hand-made but aren't, pregathered ribbons, eyelets and laces and shiny metallic braids increases. The selection of trims, braids, appliqués, rickrack, ribbons and other fabric decorations seems almost limitless.

Trims add an extra touch of personalization to your garments. Unless they are inherent to the construction of the garment, such as bias tape at raw edges (which is both a seam finish and a decorative touch), they are optional. If you've not taken the option because adding them is just one step too many, read these easy application tips. Adding trims doesn't have to add hours to the construction time for your garment. With both improved technology and easier sewing methods, adding trims no longer is a complicated process.

When you are coordinating trims with your garment, plan ahead and determine which construction method you need to use. Be sure to check washing or dry cleaning suitability, too. The trim you select usually is a permanent part of your garment and should be able to be treated in the same manner as the fabric. Preshrink trims as you do your fabric.

The easiest way to apply any trim is to apply it flat, before the final garment seam is sewn. Stitch all garment seams except one, usually the center back seam. Apply your trim and then stitch the final seam.

THE FLAT METHOD

Any trim that is finished along both edges may be applied by the flat method. Rickrack, braid, ribbon and many laces fall into this category. If you must apply trim around extremely curved edges, select bias or knit trim.

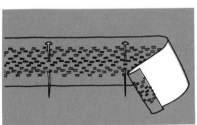

1. *Pin the trim in place, along the placement lines if you are following pattern instructions or along lines you have added if you are embellishing a pattern for an untrimmed garment.*

   After the trim is positioned accurately, finish the ends, if necessary, by turning them under 1/4" (6mm) and pressing them or holding them with a pin.

2. *If pin basting tends to ripple the trim, hand or machine baste it in place before stitching.*

Adjust the thread tension. If the stitches are too tight, the fabric underneath the trim or the trim itself could pucker. Stitch the trim, either down the center for narrow trims or rickrack or along both sides for a wider, flat trim. If a wide trim is stitched along the center only, the edges of the trim could curl up.

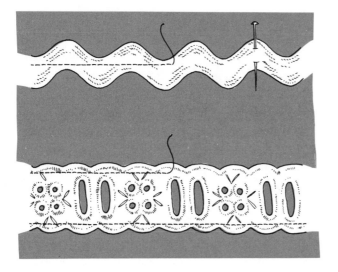

3. *When trim is going around a curve, preshape it, if it can withstand steam pressing, to match the shape of the curve to which you are applying it.*

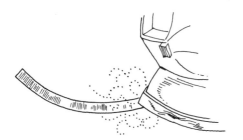

To make trim easier to handle when you are applying it to a garment, use a glue stick or fuse it instead of pinning it. To fuse, cut strips of fusible web, narrower than the trim, fuse it in place and then stitch, according to pattern directions.

———

When pre-shaping flat trims for curved areas, shape them to the **seamline**, *where they will be attached, not to the cutting line. The seamline and the cutting line may have different curves.*

4. *When trims are stitched around square corners, miter the corners for a flat, neat appearance. First, stitch the trim in place along the outside edge only, just to the point of the corner. Stop with the needle in the fabric and lift the presser foot only. Pivot the trim and fabric in the other direction.*

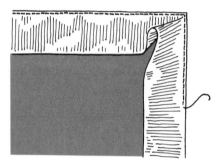

5. *Lower the presser foot and continue stitching along the edge.*

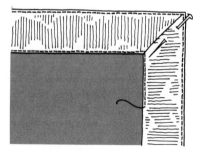

6. *Fold the excess fabric in the corner diagonally to miter it, and pin it in place. Stitch the inside edge of the trim and then finish the diagonal fold by hand or machine to hold the mitered corner in place.*

THE EDGING METHOD

Some trims are designed with one edge finished and one edge that either is inserted in a seam or is applied to the edge of the garment, often as a finishing technique. Piping, cording, fringes and many laces and eyelets are in this trim category.

1. *To apply single-edged trims along the edges of your garment, at a neckline, any opening or the bottom of a hem, for example, pin the trim to the garment along the seamline or hemline, right sides together, with the decorative edge of the trim toward the garment. Stitch the trim in place. Use a zipper foot to get close to the trim.*

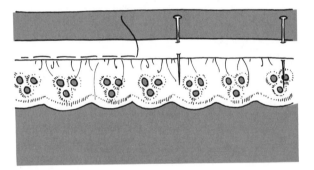

2. *If the trim end cannot be stitched in a seam, finish by using one of the following methods.*
   To finish a trim end that will be joined to another trim end, leave 1/4" (6mm) on each end for joining. After the trim is stitched in place, stitch the two trim ends together.

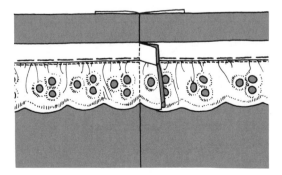

To finish a trim end that is at a finished edge, leave 1/2" (13mm) on each end. After the trim is stitched in place, turn under 1/4" (6mm), then again 1/4" (6mm) to the wrong side and slipstitch the end to finish it.

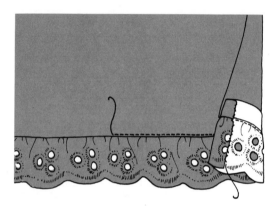

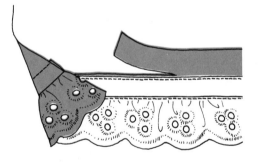

3. Finish the long edge by turning the trim seam allowance to the wrong side of your garment. Make sure the edge is even and topstitch through all thicknesses. Trim the excess fabric at the seam allowance.

TRIMS IN A SEAM

1. *If single-edged trims or flat trims, such as rickrack, are enclosed in a seam, pin the trim to the right side of one garment section, so when the seam is stitched and pressed, the outside of the trim goes in the desired direction. Place the edge to be enclosed along the* seamline, *with the decorative edge toward the body of the garment, away from the seam allowance. Most trims do not have a 5/8" (15mm) seam allowance. When you pin them along the seamline, they are stitched so the entire decoration part of the trim shows. Baste the trim in place and remove all pins (A). If rickrack is enclosed in a seam, only half the rickrack will show at the finished edge (B).*

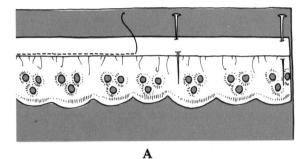

A

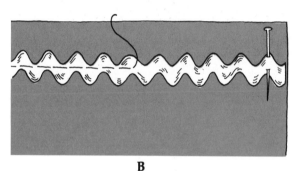

B

2. *Place the joining garment section on top of the first, right sides together, aligning the edges. The trim is between the two garment sections. Pin baste and stitch the two sections together with the trim section facing up. Stitch along the seamline, joining the three layers using the basting as a guide. Press the seam to one side, so the trim faces the desired direction. Grade the fabric seam allowances, if necessary, and turn the garment to the right side. Press along the fabric edge (C).*

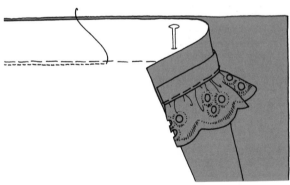

C

Waistbands

Waistline fashions on skirts and pants have taken many forms over the years, varying in width and application procedures with the variations in fashion. One easy-to-wear, easy-to-sew waistline finish is elastic in a casing. See page 115 for information on this method. Another is an applied waistband, reinforced with fusible interfacing, and a third is a faced waistline that has no waistband at all.

APPLIED

Interfacing should always be used to keep the waistband from rolling during wearing and to keep the folded edge crisp and sharp. There are two easy ways to apply an interfaced waistband and both begin with the same interfacing step using packaged, pre-cut fusible waistband interfacing. Of course, you may use regular fusible interfacing, instead. If you do, trim the interfacing 1/8" (3mm) beyond the seamlines in the seam allowance.

After cutting your fabric waistband, using one of the methods described below, place the interfacing, coated side against the wrong side of your fabric. If you are using pre-cut waistband interfacing, position the center perforations or slots along the center foldline. These interfacings are manufactured with slots so there is no extra bulk at the fold. Cover the interfacing with a damp press cloth and fuse it according to the package instructions.

The following methods for applying a waistband are easy and reduce bulk at the waistline. With the first method there will be edgestitching on the right side of the waistband. With the second, no stitching shows.

1. *One simple method for constructing a waistband uses the selvage to give you a pre-finished edge on the inside of the garment. Cut the waistband fabric with the seamline of the unnotched edge along the edge of the fabric selvage. If you are using pre-cut waist-*

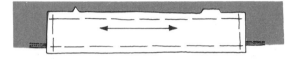

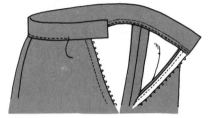

band interfacing, trim it to match the fabric waistband. Apply interfacing to the waistband. Stitch the waistband to the garment, right sides together, with the notched edge pinned to the garment. Trim the seam allowances and press the seam toward the waistband. Stitch the ends, right sides together. Trim the seam allowances and corners. Turn the waistband to the inside and secure the selvage edge along the seam with pins or fusible web. From the right side of the waistband, edgestitch close to the seamline through all layers, making sure you catch the selvage edge in the stitching, and continuing across the extended end. If desired, edgestitch all other edges.

2. *For the second method, cut the waistband with the unnotched edge along the selvage, leaving a seam allowance 3/8" (10mm) wide. You can also cut a waistband without using the selvage, but the unnotched edge should be trimmed to 3/8" (10mm) and finished with machine zigzag. If you are using pre-cut waistband interfacing, trim it to match the fabric waistband. Apply interfacing to the waistband. Stitch the waistband to the garment, right sides together, with the notched edge pinned to the garment. Trim the seam allowance and press the seam toward the waistband.*

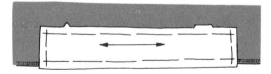

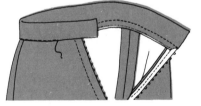

3. *With right sides together, fold the waistband along the foldline. Stitch the ends, pivoting at the corner on the extended end. On the extended end, clip diagonally on the inside of the waistband at the end of the stitching. Trim ends and corners. Turn the waistband to the inside and press. Pin the waistband in place, matching seamlines, making sure the finished edge extends 3/8" (10mm) below the seam. Tuck in the ends. "Stitch-in-the-ditch" by stitching on the outside of the garment in the ridge of the seamline, to hold the waistband in place.*

185

FACED WAISTLINES

A faced waistline may be used in place of an applied waistband. This method gives a different fit dimension to your garment, since the finished edge rests right at your waist.

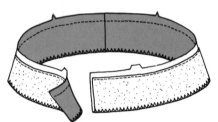

1. *Use either garment fabric or a sturdy lining fabric, which may be less bulky, for the facing. Interface the facing sections. Staystitch the facing sections along the top edge to keep them from stretching during handling.*

    Stitch the facing sections together along the short ends, leaving open the seam that will be placed at the garment opening. Press the seam allowances first the way they were stitched and then open. Trim the ends to reduce bulk. Finish the outer edge with the technique most suitable to the facing fabric. See pages 167 to 168 for information on seam finishes.

2. *Pin the facing to the garment at the waistline edge, right sides together. Match at seams and notches. Turn back the ends of the facing at the edges of your garment closure. Pin a length of ribbon seam binding to the inside of your garment, centering it over the seamline. This keeps the waistline from stretching during wearing. Because you now are working with several layers at the waistline edge, it is best to hand baste the seam tape in place, through all thicknesses, before stitching.*

    Stitch the seam through all layers, and press it as it was stitched, or flat. Grade and clip the seam allowances to permit a smooth edge.

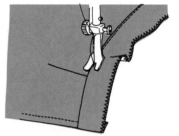

3. Lift the facing away from the garment and press all waistline seam allowances toward the facing. Understitch the seam from the right side, to keep the facing from rolling to the outside of the garment. Stitch from the right side, as close as possible to the waistline seam, through the facing and all seam allowances only.

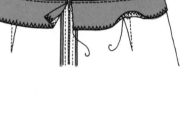

4. Turn the facing to the wrong side of your garment, helping the seamline roll slightly to the inside so it won't show on the right side. Press the facing in place along the waist edge and tack it to the garment at seams and darts to hold it.

   The facing ends should be turned under so they do not interfere with the closure. Slipstitch them in place, either to the zipper tape, if you have used a zipper, or to the seam allowance if you have used another closure method. Finish the closure with a hook and eye at the top of the waistline opening.

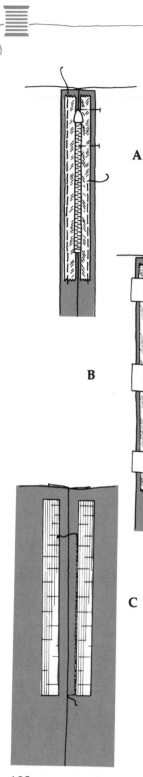

A

B

C

Zippers

CENTERED

Centered back or front zippers are zippers that look exactly the same on both long sides when they are stitched. To insert them quickly and easily, first assemble the tools you'll need—zipper foot (see page 32) and basting tape, sewing or transparent tape. For easy access to the zipper area, insert it *before* facings are attached and before the side seams of the garment are stitched. Prepare the seam into which the zipper will be inserted by basting the zipper opening closed, then backstitching at the end of the zipper opening and permanently stitching the remainder of the seam. Press the seam open.

1. *Even with a zipper foot, the zipper tape can be pushed out of line if the zipper is not secured to the seam allowances before you begin stitching. Put the right side of the closed zipper along the seam allowance with the teeth exactly on top of the basted seam. Pin, then hand baste (A) or use strips of basting or transparent tape to hold it in place (B).*

2. *Place your garment, right side up, under the zipper foot, adjusting the foot so the needle stitches about 1/4" (6mm) from the basted seam. Place sewing tape or transparent tape 1/4" (6mm) from the seam for an easy stitching guide. To keep your fabric from pulling and puckering, stitch from bottom to top on both sides of the zipper, stitching across the bottom about 1/4" (6mm) below the zipper stop (C). Remove all basting stitches.*

> *Instead of hand basting or using tape to hold a centered zipper in place for stitching, use a water-soluble glue stick instead. Apply glue to both edges of the right side of the zipper tape and finger press the zipper into position.*

MOCK FLY FRONT

A mock fly front zipper application is the easy method for achieving the look of a tailored fly front without the extra steps. Your pattern tissue will be marked for extensions that become the underlap and the overlap and that appear as wide seam allowances when folded and pressed.

1. *Stitch the center front seam from the end of the zipper marking to the symbol, or approximately the middle of the center front crotch curve. Machine baste above the zipper marking to the upper edge (A).*

2. *Turn the left front extension to the wrong side along the foldline and press. Place the closed zipper, face up, under the left front extension. Place the zipper stop at the indicated marking and keep the zipper teeth close to the fold. Baste the zipper in place, then stitch (B).*

3. *Keeping the garment front free, stitch the remaining zipper tape, face down, to the right front extension (C).*

4. *Baste the right front extension to the garment front (D).*

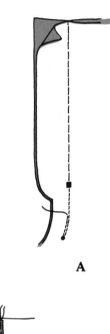

A

B   **C**   **D**

5. *On the outside, stitch the right front extension along the stitching line, through the seam allowance and zipper tape (E). To give you an accurate line to follow, place basting tape along the stitching line indicated on pattern.*

E

189

Index

191